Published by
featherproof books
Chicago, Illinois
www.featherproof.com

First edition
10 9 8 7 6 5 4 3 2 1

Library of Congress Control Number: 2014959066
ISBN 13: 978-0-9831863-3-5

Edited by Tim Kinsella and Jason Sommer.
Cover Design by Michael Renaud.
Interior Design by Zach Dodson.
Author photo by David Sampson.

Printed in the United States of America
Set in Mercury

THE FIRST COLLECTION OF CRITICISM BY A LIVING FEMALE ROCK CRITIC

JESSICA HOPPER

featherproof BOOKS

PART THREE: NOSTALGIA

PART FOUR: CALIFORNIA

PART FIVE: FAITH

PART SIX: BAD REVIEWS

PART SEVEN: STRICTLY BUSINESS

PART EIGHT: FEMALES

The title of this book is not entirely accurate. There's Ellen Willis' Beginning to See the Light, *though it wasn't all music writing, and then her posthumous collection that was. Of course Lillian Roxon's* Rock Encyclopedia *from 1969, Caroline Coon's crucial* 1988: The New Wave Punk Rock Explosion *and the collective, life-changing* Rock She Wrote. *We should be able to list a few dozen more—but those books don't exist. Yet.*

The title of this book is about planting a flag; it is for those whose dreams (and manuscripts) languished due to lack of formal precedence, support and permission. This title is not meant to erase our history but rather to help mark the path.

This book is dedicated to those that came before, those that should of been first, and all the ones that will come after.

I HAVE A STRANGE RELATIONSHIP WITH MUSIC

Hit It or Quit It #17, Spring 2002

I have a strange relationship with music. It is strange by virtue of what I need from it. Some days, it's the simple things: distraction, entertainment, the sticky joy garnered only from Timbaland beats. Then, sometimes, usually early in the part of the morning that is still night time, most especially lately, I am painfully aware of every single thing that I need from music, embarrassed by what I ask of it. Having developed such a desperate belief in the power of music to salve and heal me, I ask big, over and over again. I have an appetite for deliverance, and am not really interested in trying to figure out whether it qualifies me as lucky or pathetic.

The stereo is just past halfway to as-loud-as-it-will-go, the rolling bass of Van Morrison's "T.B. Sheets" (the first song on side two of the album of the same name) is moving throughout the house, its punctuating bump'n'grind ricocheting off the parquet floor, sound filling every room. This makes the fourth night in the last five that I'm doing this same routine—lights out, alone, in a precarious emotional state not worth explaining, dancing, though in a way that is barely dancing, because lying down is out of the question on a night as hot as this, and lying down means motionless, and there's really no being still right now.

T.B. Sheets is a great album on which seven of the eight songs are about Van Morrison and a girl he loves, who is dying of tuberculosis. I can count on one hand the times that I have made it through the entire album without crying. It's brutal and never fails to deliver in its relentless humanity. Some songs detail the recent past, a golden reminiscence of some then-average day ("Who Drove the Red Sports Car") that now will have to be enough for a lifetime; he's asking her, *"Do you remember?"* insinuating some intimate exchange, some forgotten little secret. He needs her to remember. "Beside You" is a fierce, rambling pledge—he's pleading for her confidence, in a torrential cadence of nearly unintelligible half-sentences that sound like they could be directions someplace, before the decimating crescendo. He sounds drunk, a little off-key, hysterical, now saying everything he ever meant to say to her and didn't, confessing himself, as if this act of deathbed desperation, this unbearable love, this compassion to the point of oneness with her, if she knew it, if she could really understand it, and take it in—it might just save her. All of this is cast out amongst ominous, trilling B3 sustain and repetitive guitar, droning off into bottomless tension. (A version of this song appears later on, a version which is totally chardonnay and mystic gamelan flutes and angelic production, in comparison to the decidedly drinkin'-straight-from-the-bottle, succulent, lo-fi, four-bar, party-blues hip sway of the original.)

The title track, "T.B. Sheets," is nine minutes and 44 seconds of Van rending an exquisite topography of bleak human expanse, an outline of him collapsing under the weight of incontrovertible mortal pall, in a dialect too casual and acrimonious for how well he knows her. He's unable to be of any use—unable to get far away fast enough from his fear, evading the knowledge of exactly what all this means, the finality of it. Details give way to a much deeper reckoning: "I can almost smell / The T.B. sheets." Audibly choking for air, and again repeating, with frail cogency, "I gotta go" over and over, like a mantra of absolution, seeking another set of chances, burdened by survival.

But it's too late, he's in for all he's got.

It's a song of failure. It's realizing that sometimes the best you've got to give isn't much of anything at all.

Dancing in pitch-dark rooms, rooms illuminated exclusively by the tiny light on the turntable, is an activity which fits very well with my ideas of "rock-critic behavior" (which is like normal music-fan behavior, but substantially more pitiful and indulgent). It's behavior that comes from an inextricable soul-entanglement with music that is insular, boundless, devoted, celebratory and willfully pathetic. It's my fantasized notion of what a REAL rock-critic scenario is like: a "special" manual typewriter, ashtrays full of thin roaches, an extensive knowledge of Mott the Hoople lyrics, a ruthless seeking for the life of life in free jazz sides. May also include: a fetishizing of THE TRUTH (which always turns gory, no matter what records you listen to), detoured attempts to illuminate the exact heaven of Eric B. & Rakim or Rocket from the Tombs with the fluorescent lighting of yr 3 a.m. genius stroke prose; and, most of all, an insatiable appetite for rapture that cannot be coaxed by any other means. And oh what motherfucking deliverance when you find it! It's exhaustively chronicling what it is that artists possess that we mere mortals do not; what it is that they offer up that we are unable or unwilling to say ourselves. They offer a connection to the disconnected, they make our secrets bearable in their verses and choruses: ornate in their undoing, gambling with their happiness, their personal irredemption, their humility, using failure to build a podium to reach god, their faked orgasms amid in-between-song skits, their solos, their clever rhymes, their crippled expectations, their spiritual drift, their still-unmet Oedipal needs, their fuckless nights, their not not-so-gradual disappearance from reality, their rodeo blues, their ghetto living/ghetto dying, their unflagging romantic beliefs, of being an outlaw for your love, Reaganomics, the summer they'll never forget, the power of funk, hanging at the Nice Nice w/ the eye patch guy, American apathy, taking hoes to the Cheesecake Factory, getting head in drop-top Benzes, isolation, the benefits of capitalism, screwing Stevie Nicks in the tall green grass, the swirling death dust, the underground and none of the above.

I want it. I need it. Because all these records, they give me a language to decipher just how fucked I am. Because there is a void in my guts which can only be filled by songs.

PART ONE

CHICAGO

EMO: WHERE THE GIRLS AREN'T
Punk Planet #56, July 2003

A few months back, I was at a Strike Anywhere show. The band launched into "Refusal," a song that offers solidarity with the feminist movement and bears witness to the struggles inherent to women's lives. It is not a song of protection, there is no romantic undertow, it's just about all people being equally important. Everyone was dancing, fanboys and girls at the lip of the stage screaming along— like so many shows at the Fireside. By the first chorus of the song, I was in tears with a sudden awareness: I've been going to three shows a week for the last decade and the number of times I've heard women's reality acknowledged or portrayed in a song sung by male-fronted band was at zero and holding. This song was the first.

It's no wonder why my girlfriends and I have grown increasingly alienated and distanced from the scene, or have begun taking shelter from emo's pervasive stronghold in the recesses of electronic, DJ or experimental music. No wonder girls I know are feeling dismissive and faithless towards music. No wonder I feel much more allegiance to MOP's "Ante Up" than any song by an all-dude band about the singer's romantic holocaust. Because as it stands in 2003 I simply cannot substantiate the effort it takes to give a flying fuck about the genre/plague that we know as emo or myopic songs that don't consider the world beyond boy bodies, their broken hearts or their vans. Meanwhile, we're left wondering—how did we get here?

As hardcore and political punk's charged sentiments became more cliché towards the end of the '80s and we all began slipping to into the armchair comfort of the Clinton era—punk stopped looking outward and began stripping off its tough skin only and examine its squishy heart instead, forsaking songs about the impact of trickle down economics for ones about elusive kisses. Mixtapes across America became laden with relational eulogies—hopeful boys with their hearts masted to sleeves, their pillows soaked in tears. Punk's songs became personal, often myopically so.

Perhaps we lost the map, or simply stopped consulting it. There was a time when emo seemed reasonable, encouraging, exciting—revivifying in its earnestness and personal stakes. These new bands modeled themselves on bands we all liked: Jawbox, Jawbreaker, Sunny Day Real Estate. The difference was, in those bands' songs about women, the girls had names, details to their lives. Jawbox's most popular song, "Savory," was about recognizing male normative privilege, about the weight of objectification on a woman ("See you feign surprise / That I'm all eyes"). In Jawbreaker songs, women had leverage, had life, had animus and agency to them. Sometimes they were friends, or a sister, not always a girl to be bedded or dumped by. They were unidealized, realistic characters.

And then something broke—and not just Mr. Dashboard's sensitive heart. Records by a legion of romantically-wronged boys suddenly lined the record store shelves. Every record was seemingly a concept album about a breakup, damning the girl on the other side. Emo's contentious monologues—these balled-fist, Peter Pan mashnote dilemmas—have now gone from being descriptive to being prescriptive. Emo has become another forum where women were locked out, observing ourselves through the eyes of others.

Girls in emo songs today do not have names. We are not identified beyond our absence, our shape drawn by the pain we've caused. Our lives, our day-to-day-to-day does not exist, we do not get colored in. Our actions are portrayed solely through the detailing of neurotic self-entanglement of the boy singer—our region of personal power, simply, is our impact on his romantic life. We're vessels redeemed in the light of boy-love. On a pedestal, on our backs. Muses at best. Cum rags or invisible at worst. Check out our pictures on the covers of records—we are sad-eyed and winsome and comely (thank you Hot Rod Circuit, The Crush, Cursive, Something Corporate, et al.)— the fantasy girl you could take home and comfort.

It's evident from these bands' lyrics and shared aesthetic that their knowledge of actual living, breathing women is notional at best. Emo's characteristic vulnerabile front is limited to self-sensitivity, every song a high-stakes game of control that involves "winning" or "losing" possession of the girl (see Dashboard Confessional, Brand New, New Found Glory and Glassjaw albums for prime examples). Yet, in the vulnerability there is no empathy, no peerage or parallelism. Emo's yearning doesn't connect it with women—it omits them.

As Andy Greenwald notes in his book about emo culture, *Nothing*

Feels Good: Punk Rock, Teenagers and Emo, lyrically, emo singers "revel in their misery and suffering to an almost ecstatic degree, but with a limited use of subtlety and language. It tends to come off like Rimbaud relocated to the Food Court." Women in emo songs are denied the dignity of humanization through both the language and narratives, we are omnipresent yet chimerical, only of consequence in romantic settings.

***

On a dance floor in Seattle, a boy I know decides to plumb the topic:

"I heard you're writing a column about how emo is sexist."

"I am."

"What do you mean '*emo is sexist*'? Emo songs are no different than all of rock history, than Rolling Stones or Led Zeppelin."

"I know—I'd rather not get into right now."

"How are songs about breaking up sexist though? Everyone breaks up. If you have a problem with emo, you have a problem with all of rock history!"

"I know. I do."

To paraphrase Nixon sidekick H.R. Haldeman, "History is wack."

There must be some discussion, at least for context, about the well-worn narrative of the boy rebel's broken heart, as exemplified by the last fifty-plus years of blues-based music, that there are songs about loving and losing women; that *men writing songs about women* is practically the definition of rock 'n' roll. And as a woman, as a music critic, as someone who lives and dies for music, there is a rift within, a struggle of how much deference you can afford, and how much you are willing to ignore what happens in these songs simply because you like the music.

Can you ignore the lyrical content of the Stones' "Under my Thumb" because you like the song? Are you willing to? Or the heaping pile of dead or brutalized women that amasses in Big Black's discography? Is emo exceptional in the scope of the rock canon either in terms of treatment of women or in its continual rubbing salute to its own trouble-boy cliché image? Is there anything that separates Dashboard Confessional's condemnation of his bed-hopping betrayer and makes it any more egregious than any woman/mother/whore/ex-girlfriend showing up in songs of Jane's Addiction, Nick Cave, The Animals or Justin Timberlake? Can you forgo judgment woe to women in the recorded catalog of Zeppelin because the first eight bars of "Communication Breakdown" is total fucking godhead? Where do you split? Do you even bother to care, because if you're going to try and kick against it, you, as my dancing friend says, "have a problem with all of rock history," and because who, other than a petty, too-serious bitch dismisses Zeppelin?! Do you accept the sexism and phallocentricity of the last few decades of popular music and in your punk rock community as just how it is?

Who do you excuse and why? Do you check your politics at the door and just dance or just rock or just let side A spin out? Can you ignore the marginalization of women's lives on the records that line your record shelves in hopes that feigned ignorance will bridge the gulf, because it's either that or purge your collection of everything but free jazz, micro house 12"s and the Mr. Lady Records catalog?

It's almost too big of a question to ask. I start to ask this of myself, to really start investigating, and stop, realizing full well that if I get an answer I might just have to retire to an adobe hut in the Italian countryside and not take any visitors for a long time. Or turn into the rock critical Andrea Dworkin, and report with resignation that all music made by men propagates the continual oppression and domination of women. Sometimes I feel like every rock song I hear is a sucker punch towards us. And I feel like no one takes that impact seriously, let alone notices it. It is "just" music.

My deepest concerns about the lingering effects of emo is not so much for myself or for my friends—we have refuge in our personal-political platforms and deep-crated record collections—but rather for the teenage girls I see crowding front and center at emo shows. The ones who for whom this is their inaugural introduction to the underground, whose gateway may have been through Weezer or the Vagrant America tour or maybe Dashboard Confessional's *Un-*

plugged. The ones who are seeking music out, who are wanting to stake some claim to punk rock, or an underground avenue, for a way out, a way under, to sate the seemingly unquenchable, nameless need—the same need I know I came to punk rock with. Emo is the province of the young, their foundation is fresh-laid, my concern is for people who have no other previous acquaintance with the underground, save for these bands and their songs.

When I was that age, I too had a hunger for a music that spoke a language I was just starting to decipher, music that affirmed my ninth grade fuck-you values—music that encouraged me to not allow my budding feminist ways to be bludgeoned by the weight of mainstream, patriarchal culture—I was lucky I was met at the door with things like the Bikini Kill demo, Fugazi and the first Kill Rock Stars comp. I was met with polemics and respectful address; I heard my life and concerns in those songs. I was met with girl heroes deep in guitar squall, kicking out the jams under the stage lights. I was being hurtled towards deeper rewards. Records and bands were triggering ideas and inspiration. I acknowledge the importance of all of that because I know I would not be who I am now, doing what I do, 12 years down the line, if I had not had gotten those fundamentals, been presented with those big ideas about what music and, moreover, what life, can be about.

So now I watch these girls at emo shows more than I ever do the band. I watch them sing along, to see what parts they freak out over. I wonder if this does it for them, if seeing these bands, these dudes on stage, resonates and inspires them to want to pick up a guitar or drum sticks. Or if they just see this as something dudes do, since there are no girls, there is no *them* up there. I wonder if they see themselves as participants, or only as consumers or—if we reference the songs directly—the consumed. I wonder if this is where music will begin and end for them. If they can be radicalized in spite of this. If being denied keys to the clubhouse is enough to spur them into action.

I know that, for me, even as a teenage autodidact who thought her every idea was worthy of expression and an audience, it did not occur to me to start a band until I saw other women in one. It took seeing Babes in Toyland and Bikini Kill to truly throw on the lights, to show me that there was more than one place, one role, for women to occupy, and that our participation was important and vital—it was YOU MATTER writ large.

I don't want these front row girls to miss that. I don't want girls leaving clubs denied of encouragement and potential. As lame as punk rock can be, as hollow as all of our self-serving claims ring—that the culture of punk is truly different somehow than that of median society—at its gnarled foundations still exists the possibilities for connection. There is still the possibility for exposure to radical notions, for punk rock to match up to what many kids dream, or hope for punk DIY to mean. But much of that hinges on the continual presence of radicalized women within the leagues, and those women being encouraged—given reasons to stay, to want to belong—rather than diminished by the music which glues the community together.

Us girls deserve more than one song. We deserve more than one pledge of solidarity. We deserve better songs than any boy will ever write about us.

CHANCE THE RAPPER

A truncated version ran in *Chicago Magazine*, June 2013

Chance the Rapper doesn't want to go home. He just came from there, he says. The 20-year old rapper is in the passenger seat of my car. We were slated to drive around his South Side neighborhood, Chatham, where he grew up and now lives with his girlfriend. There are a flurry of excuses: It's hot out. It will take too long and he has to be at the studio in an hour. The 'hood where he lives is just where he lives, he says. His story, of how he went from half-dropped-out burner kid to Chicago's next big thing, he insists, "happened here." He motions to indicate that *here* means exactly where we are—this few-block stretch of downtown surrounding the Harold Washington branch of the Chicago Public Library.

Despite his casual air and congenial charm, Chance is very aware of his image, his origin story and how much it constitutes his appeal. Beneath his earnest demeanor lies a kid who has mapped every inch of his hustle. Chance is a favorite with high school kids, in part, because his story could be theirs. He paints himself as the one kid amid the overachievers at Jones Prep who did not care about his future. Likable but a loner, he got busted smoking weed while ditching class at Millennium Park and spent his subsequent 10-day suspension recording a mixtape of songs that birthed his rap career. His is a ground-level stardom, someone kids can touch and talk to when they see him on the train or in the street—he is someone they could ostensibly become. The young MC is very clear on the importance of his apocryphal tale and that is the only one he is inclined to tell. And so we will not begin our story of Chance the Rapper in Chatham, we will begin where he says it began: downtown.

We park and step out of the car outside of the Columbia College dorms. There is the waft of marijuana and someone yells "Whattup, man!" A former classmate from Jones appears and pulls Chance in for a half-hug, and explains, "He was the craziest motherfucker in school!" The old friend passes Chance his joint. Chance plugs his upcoming mixtape by name and street date. They exchange numbers after the kid offers his in case Chance needs a hookup for weed.

It is difficult to ascertain whether Chance is famous citywide, but in this six-block proximity of where we walk, he is the Mayor of the Underage. He is greeted constantly, by name, with handshakes, pounds, dap. He gamely poses for pictures, is offered lights for his ever-present cigarettes, and kids prod his memory to see if he remembers the last time they met—at the library, in the parking lot of their school when he was selling tickets to one of his shows, that one time their cousin introduced them.

We head down the street to Juggrnaut, the hip-hop clothing store that has hosted all of Chance's mixtape release parties, drawing hundreds more kids than they can accommodate in the tiny space. Owner Roger Rodriguez brags that they've known him since back when he was "Just Chance. Before he was Chance *Thee*." In the store, the half dozen dudes shopping look up but play it like they are not noticing Chance, who refers to the store as "home." He would sometimes spend six hours a day there, writing rhymes or just hanging out. That doesn't really happen anymore. Two middle school-age boys in uniforms pass by and pause to gawk when they catch sight of Chance through the open door. Chance gives them an acknowledging wave. They wave back before running away.

After Juggrnaut, we head east on Washington and make a left on State and head into the YouMedia center on the ground floor of the library. "The first time I came here was to rap," he explains. Kanye-obsessed Chance was in a duo with a friend ("We were terrible") and had heard that the library had free recording studios. The center also offers free workshops; "Production, software, piano lessons, music theory—I took all of them." He quickly became the star of the popular Wednesday-night open mics. "This place made me what I am today." He swings open the door to the recording studio and pops his head in. Five teenage boys are inside, one is behind the mic, the rest behind the computer. "Y'all recording?" he asks. "I used to be recording in here—I don't mean to hold up your session." Chance acts oblivious but the boys are stunned silent. This is a little like Derrick Rose suddenly sidling up while you're free-throwing in the driveway.

By the time he ducks back out a minute later, nearly a dozen boys have amassed in a semicircle. "All y'all rap?" he asks them. They all giddily introduce themselves by names they rap under. Dre Valentine, E-Man, Vic-Ivy, Psycho Ten Times. The iPhones come out and there is a group shot. They are all 15, 16, 17—the same age as Chance when he started camping out at YouMedia—and all of them are from the Chicago's South Side, too. A kid who raps as Esh explains, "Everyone knows this is where Chance made *10 Day*." We decide to leave, as it becomes apparent that every kid in the library has realized *Chance is here*.

Within the next half block he is stopped and recognized by the a janitor from Jones Prep, he takes pictures with three girls he knows from YouMedia, the cousin of his DJ and three rappers he knows from street ciphers. I ask one of them, Pres, why Chance's success is so important to Chicago. "Everyone feel like he's on his way up. He's the voice of the youth in the Chi—but he is just part of it. He's the lightbearer."

VIVA LA FILTHY NOISE!: COUGHS' *SECRET PASSAGE*

Chicago Reader, **October 2006**

Every time Coughs count off a song it's like a ticking toward detonation; every show they play is rumored to be their last, threatening both explosion and implosion. These locals' most recent "last show" was last month at the Empty Bottle, during *The Wire*'s Adventures in Modern Music fest, and their fiercely kinetic cacophony was as tight as it's ever been, awing and frightening an already timid crowd. (People who can afford a $15 cover are not Coughs' usual demographic.) The audience formed a polite arc at a safe distance from the stage, but the band refused them their distance—only four of the six members stayed behind their monitors. Front woman Anya Davidson took to the floor, shuffling around like an expiring windup toy, her eyes shut, bumping gently but obliviously into people as she screamed out a dialogue with a talking pimple ("Life of Acne"). And keyboardist and saxophonist Jail Flanagan barreled into the front row, charging ass first into the laps of the people sitting on the steps as she blew sick, squalling runs. You could almost see what the crowd was thinking: *These people are wet with sweat and stink and they are trying to touch us.*

Coughs use every instrument as a percussion instrument, not just the trashed, monolithic two-man megakit at the back of the stage—a multicolored heap of snares, cymbals, soup pots, floor toms, metal barrels, and bass drums mounted flat like tabletops. The guitar and bass pile on with more banging and chomping, and even the vocals and saxophone steer clear of melody—the songs could be sketched out with only two or three symbols, one for the thuds and another couple for the breaks and scree between the thuds. There's little that compares to the sound Coughs make, unless you abandon bands as points of reference: it's like a massive conglomeration of screeching worn-out cab brakes, assembly-line machines, and pneumatic nail guns, the whole thing driven by the maniacally rapid heartbeat of a small mammal. The closest aesthetic antecedents are either early Boredoms or a car crash.

On their new album, *Secret Passage* (Load), they play like they're trying to tear apart the songs themselves and maybe take down whoever's listening as well. But the mushroom cloud rising from this destruction has a silver lining—the explosion is more like the Big Bang, and it feels like something huge is happening inside that bubble of blast heat. Coughs' intensity makes them seem bigger and more important than just a band; they stand for the destruction of contemporary pop with all its rote prescriptions and attendant soul death. They're a cleansing fire purging the earth of the swagger of the Stones, the tired aggro posturing of punk and hardcore, the vapid "I can't live without you"'s of R&B—their music clears a space for the clever-whatever that's coming in their wake. Direct and unmediated, not referencing much of anything, it's at times purposefully ugly, even gloriously so. But the fury doesn't come out of hate; it's pure-hearted, boldly altruistic. On their Myspace page, the "Sounds Like" box says "genres collapsing." That is in fact what they sound like, and they're doing us a favor: lighting a path out, delivering us to the future via filthy noise.

When I saw Coughs play for the first time this spring, I was filled with prommy sentiment: I leaned and yelled into the side of my best friend's head, "I don't want this night to ever end." But I've also seen the band bring out the worst in an audience, usually when some deeply-damaged Reagan babies try to up Coughs' ante with extra insolence. This summer at a Coughs show in some crumbly warehouse, I watched a modelescent girl with long golden tresses and expensively wrong clothes stand amid the surging crowd and carefully hock gobs of spit onto Davidson. The girl's pupils were pinpricks and she had blood on her face, like she'd gone over her handlebars on the way to the show. But she couldn't add to the chaos or top the damage Davidson had already done to herself: her too-small dress was shredding and slipping off her as she heaved, screaming, her hands pulling at the nest of her hair.

The way Davidson acts is just not how you ever see women present themselves in bands. Even when the most ferocious and confident women perform, there's almost always an allusion to the expectations they're sidestepping—to come across as "bad girls," they need the rules hovering close at hand. But Davidson doesn't seem aware those rules ever existed—half the time she doesn't even seem aware of the audience. I've never seen a woman so naturally give less of a fuck. You could call it feminist if she seemed more conscious of what she's doing—it's like she was dropped here by aliens and never suffered the USA damage that makes girls kowtow involuntarily to the watchful eyes of convention. She's our very own Iggy, unzipping her pants to expose the delicate print of some Hanes Her Ways as beer drips from her hair, howling like Patti Smith if she'd come up on bunk acid and small-town metal bands instead of blues and Baudelaire. She's Niki de Saint Phalle, riddling her canvas with bullet holes out of love and rage.

The other members of the band—a motley, Bad News Bears assortment—are hardly cookie-cutter personalities themselves. Percussionists Jon Ziemba and Seth Sher play standing up, often shirtless, like they're trying to beat their way out from behind the piled-up barricade of their gear with constant colossal rolls and the martial rattle of a meth-powered high school marching band. Guitarist Vanessa Harris, who often sports a crooked coonskin hat, is the band's melodic glue, though that's not saying much—air-raid-siren squeals and one-note unsolos are her specialty. Bassist Carrie Vinarsky dresses like a hausfrau—last time I saw her she was wearing a turtleneck, high-waisted pleat-front jeans, and an embroidered vest— but her bass tone is so punishingly swampy it'd make the guy from Killdozer jealous.

Coughs began in 2001 as a cross between an experiment and a dare—no one in the band was allowed to play an instrument she already knew how to play. Their earlier recordings are rippin', but their haphazard spazziness makes them sound like the product of an accident rather than a collective aesthetic decision. From its first atonal bleat, by contrast, *Secret Passage* pounces with a purposeful ferocity. Coughs' wretched, razor-sharp skronking still has a home-made charm but now it has a keen and assaultive focus, proving that they've figured out how to engage their instruments for maximum damage. Their early insistence on learning as they went has made their playing more idiosyncratic and unsettling as they've developed chops—though "chops" is a relative term, of course, and in this case it just means they can stomp and churn in unison when they want to.

Secret Passage is also a joyous record, positive and uplifting, despite its calamitous clanging and murder screams. Davidson may sing like she's trying to punch a hole through a wall with her voice, but her lyrics are genuine, colored with a strange innocence. You'd never guess, watching her force every ounce of air from her lungs till she's beet red, that she's screaming about mountains, birds, dreams, gardening, freedom, or pining for a lover who arrives on goatback. On "15 Hole," when she barks *"Je suis bombe atomique,"* it's as much a promise as a threat.

SWEET THINGS

Village Voice Pazz & Jop Critics Poll, January 2006

Dear Sufjan,

I enjoyed your new album about my city and state and I am wondering if you are available, one day soon—perhaps when you are less busy being a newly famous Christian troubadour—to drive around Chicago and listen to "Sweet Thing" by Van Morrison over and over, and see who cries first, you or me. I do not know what "losing" would consist of—crying first or not crying. It wouldn't be a date or anything weird like that, just a friendly contest. Then I could show you the cool things around town that you did not sing about on your record. We could drive under the Green Line tracks where a car chase from *The Blues Brothers* took place, visit the fern room at the Garfield Park Conservatory, the top-floor atrium of the Harold Washington Library where the floors are marble and cool and very clean and no one is ever there so you can lay on them and look up into the downtown sky or just read the books you checked out, the Soul Vegetarian vegan soul food restaurant run by the African Hebrew Israelites, the Baha'i temple in Wilmette which gets a lot of god in the architecture and is ringed with seven gardens. If you aren't scared of dark, isolated places there is always the train-line land bridge that runs through the industrial corridor to downtown where there are tons of baby rabbits and great discarded things—last time I was up there there was part of an old fair ride and the sign for a mid-'60s hair salon with fluttering, sequiny letters. We could sneak onto the elevators at the Drake Hotel and look at the lake at night—and if it's fall they have apples in baskets in the hallways that are for decoration, but if you are me, they are for stealing and eating.

Maybe you wrote songs about that stuff for your Illinois record, but they did not fit on the album, or the choruses were weak, or the song about Decatur was more fun to sing because of those half-funny half-rhymes ("aviator?!"). If you did not already write those songs, you are going to wish you had.

Yours very truly,
JH
Chicago, Illinois

AND WE REMAIN,
EVER SO FAITHFULLY, YOURS

TINYLUCKYGENIUS, January 2006

What you forget when you do not drink, when you do not hit the bars on the weekend, when you are not on the streets as the good-timing people float or straggle out; what you forget is the particular sound of drunken Midwestern girls with that high Cicero shine to their voices, so sharp it can cut through the sound of a downpour a half block away. Heeled boots stutter-scraping along, keep slopping clip-cloppity time to her liquid chattering that pierces.

It is on my short list of why I will one day move to the woods. Nothing is grosser than people after last call. I want barn owls in their place.

My night was long. It is sometimes strangely lonely doing stories, out by yourself, glued to the makeshift notepad, noticing, noticing, scribbling blindly, looking for the point of interest. But on the way there, to those points of interest, that may or may not be of actual interest until they matriculate and get interpreted when you are typing it all up hours later, en route, there are bands that feel like violence and punks who vomit on the floor like it is their job. There are people that laugh at vomiting punx, then there are those that stifle a gag, then there are those of us grateful our purse is made of rubber as beer and gyro meat flecks its side, as it rains from the singer of the Functional Blackouts' mouth, in between choruses, for the third time.

Tonight, point of interest, was ladies' mud wrestling in an abandoned warehouse. People were contained to one room, with a bathroom line so long people were pissing in hallways and out-of-the-way spots, hawking for a good spot from which to best eye some exposed, muddied titty. After 40 minutes in one room, everyone was acting ratty, idling, as it was past capacity, and the wrestler-folks were limiting the amount of people in the wrestling room because the floor was weak, structurally. There was no heat and it was BYOB and by 11 p.m., a third of the room was pirate-eyed, slack-faced, screaming and rowdy, tired of waiting through bands, demanding wrestling honeys now. Twenty minutes later, I was sandwiched between a mudcaked pansexual orgy in the front row and a sea of dudes making comments about every wrestling girl, every move, what every leopard-print bra discarded in the ring amidst the chaos exposed. All 70 of the dudes cheered and clucked when the ref would instruct the girls to get on their knees at the start of the rounds. I think, in times like this, with my ear cocked to all this bullshit, that such greed is our most natural nature. To consume with appetite infinite—never satiable. My humanity stiffens—reporting this, writing this out means I have to process it, I have to take it all in, and it feels like a burden.

I concentrated on my notes and tried to duck when the ref slam'd his hand into the mud when he did the pinning counts—it sent the mud arcing through the room in threes.

The final round, where a lucky raffle-winner boy from the audience wrestled two girls, was overtaken by an audience-on-audience mud fight. I scrawled long notes about the scrawny boy, clad in a thong, joyfully allowing himself to be pinned, his shameless boner like a gift to the world, mud caking his smile. When it was over, I turned my shirt inside out so not to endanger my still pristine Paddington yellow coat, which I had hid far from the vomiting, beerspilling and mudsplatting. I headed out, passed the cops and rollergirls and boys talking about asses and bands, and went outside, walked a few blocks and waited for the bus. Stupidly, I assumed with all the mud soaking my hair and much of my face and being that I was dressed like a child in a story book, in my wader boots and canary coat, and that I was seated at a bus stop—you know, I thought that I did not look like I was out to turn tricks... but alas, no. I forgot, if you are a girl outdoors after midnight on a weekend, you might as well put groundeffects around your pussy. A dude in a Benz, a cabbie, and another dude cruising his sparkletrash with a spoiler—a woodbead crucifix from the rearview—all sought me for some service. I didn't react in the way I used to when I was a young woman, which was get close enough and then spit in their faces. Instead I watched the muffler shop's sign blink from time to temperature, time to temperature for 23 minutes until the 77 showed.

The first bus was full of muddy people screaming each others' names for no reason.

The second bus I got on, a girl was rolling on her boyfriend, nuzzling, muting him with her whole body, her words were past slurring, just some grunting whine; turns out she just wanted a kiss.

CONVERSATION WITH JIM DEROGATIS REGARDING R. KELLY

The Village Voice, **December 2013**

It has been nearly 15 years since music journalist Jim DeRogatis caught the story that has since defined his career, one that he wishes didn't exist: R. Kelly's sexual predation on teenage girls. DeRogatis, at that time the pop-music critic at the *Chicago Sun-Times,* was anonymously delivered the first of two videos he would receive depicting the pop star engaging in sexual acts with underage girls. Now the host of the syndicated public radio show *Sound Opinions* and a professor at Columbia College, DeRogatis, along with his former *Sun-Times* colleague Abdon Pallasch, didn't just break the story, they did the only significant reporting on the accusations against Kelly, interviewing hundreds of people over the years, including dozens of young women whose lives DeRogatis says were ruined by the singer.

This past summer, leading up to Kelly's headlining performance at the Pitchfork Music Festival, DeRogatis posted a series of discussions about Kelly's career, the charges made against him, and sexual assault. He published a live review of the singer's festival set that was an indictment of Pitchfork and its audience for essentially endorsing a man he calls "a monster." In the two weeks since Kelly released his latest studio album, *Black Panties,* the conversation about him and why he has gotten a pass from music publications (not to mention feminist sites such as Jezebel) has been rekindled, in part because of the explicit nature of the album and also because of online arguments around the Pitchfork performance.

I was one of those people who challenged DeRogatis and was even flip about his judgment—something I quickly came to regret. DeRogatis and I have tangled—even feuded on air—over the years; yet, amid the Twitter barbs, he approached me offline and told me about how one of Kelly's victims called him in the middle of the night after his Pitchfork review came out, to thank him for caring when no one else did. He told me of mothers crying on his shoulder, seeing the scars of a suicide attempt on a girl's wrists, the fear in their eyes. He detailed an aftermath that the public has never had to bear witness to.

DeRogatis offered to give me access to every file and transcript he has collected in reporting this story—as he has to other reporters and journalists, none of whom has ever looked into the matter, thus relegating it to one man's personal crusade.

I thought that last fact merited a public conversation about why.

In this interview (which has been condensed significantly), DeRogatis speaks frankly and explicitly about the many disturbing charges against Kelly and says, ultimately, "The saddest fact I've learned is nobody matters less to our society than young black women. Nobody."

Refresh our memories. How did this start for you?

Being a beat reporter, music critic at a Chicago daily, the *Sun-Times*, R. Kelly was a huge story for me, this guy who rose from not graduating from Kenwood Academy, singing at backyard barbecues and on the L, to suddenly selling millions of records. I interviewed him a number of times. Then *TP2.com* came out. I'd written a review that said the jarring thing about Kelly is that one moment he wants to be riding you and then next minute he's on his knees, crying and praying to his dead mother in heaven for forgiveness for his unnamed sins. It's a little weird at times. It's just an observation.

The next day at the *Sun-Times*, we got this anonymous fax—we didn't know where it came from. It said: R. Kelly's been under investigation for two years by the sex-crimes unit of the Chicago police. And I threw it on the corner of my desk. I thought, "playerhater." Now, from the beginning, there were rumors that Kelly likes them young. And there'd been this Aaliyah thing—*Vibe* printed, without much commentary and no reporting, the marriage certificate. Kelly or someone had falsified her age as 18. There was that. So all this is floating in the air. This fax arrives and I think, "Oh, this is somebody playing with this." But there was something that nagged at me as a reporter. There were specific names, specific dates, and those great, long, Polish cop names. And you're not going to make that crap up. So I went to the city desk and I asked, "What do we do with this?" They said, Abdon Pallasch is the courts reporter, why don't you two look into it and see if there's anything there? And it turns out there had been lawsuits that had been filed that had never been reported.

When you cover the courts in Chicago or any city, you go twice a day and you go through the bin of cases that have been filed and every once in a while Michael Jordan's been sued or someone went bankrupt and it's this sexy story and you pull it out. These suits had been filed at 4 p.m. on Christmas Eve. Ain't no reporter working at 4 p.m. on Christmas Eve, and they flew under the radar. So we had these lawsuits that were explosive and we didn't understand why nobody had reported them.

Explosive in what regard?

They were stomach-churning. The one young woman, who had been 14 or 15 when R. Kelly began a relationship with her, detailed in great length, in her affidavits, a sexual relationship that began at Kenwood Academy: He would go back in the early years of his success and go to Lena McLin's gospel choir class. She's a legend in Chicago, gospel royalty. He would go to her sophomore class and hook up with girls afterward and have sex with them. Sometimes buy them a pair of sneakers. Sometimes just letting them hang out in his presence in the recording studio. She detailed the sexual relationship that she was scarred by. It lasted about one and a half to two years, and then he dumped her and she slit her wrists, tried to kill herself. Other girls were involved. She recruited other girls. He picked up other girls and made them all have sex together. A level of specificity that was pretty disgusting.

Her lawsuit was hundreds of pages long, and Kelly countersued. The countersuit was, like, 10 pages long: "None of this is true!" We began our reporting. We knocked on a lot of doors. The lawsuits, the two that we had found initially, had been settled. Kelly had paid the women and their families money and the settlements were sealed by the court. But of course, the initial lawsuits remain part of the public record.

So her affidavit, this testimony—it's all public record?

To this day, any reporter who so cares can go to Cook County and pull these records, so it drives me crazy, even with some of the eloquent reconsiderations we've seen of Kelly in recent days, that they keep saying "rumors" and "allegations." Well, "allegations" is fair, OK. You're protected as a reporter, any lawsuit that has been filed as fact. The contents of the lawsuit are protected. So these were not rumors. These were allegations made in court.

Do you think part of how it's been handled and why it's been underreported is that music writers may not know how to deal with it in a journalistic sense?

Let's start with the most mundane part. A lot of people who are critics are fans and don't come with any academic background, with any journalistic background, research background. Now, nobody knows everything, and far be it from me to say you've got to be a journalist or you have to have studied critical theory in the academy. Part of what we do is journalistic. Get the names right, get the dates right, get the facts right. Sometimes, on a very rare number of stories, there's a deeper level of reporting required.

There's another reason: People are squeamish. I think a lot of people don't know how to do it, don't care to do it, and it's way too much work. It's just kind of disgusting to have to write about this and bum everyone out when you just want to review a record.

You and I got into it over Twitter around Pitchfork, in part over the fact that you were saying, "If you are enjoying R. Kelly, you're effectively co-signing what this man has done." At the time, I was being defensive, saying people can like what they like.

To be clear, I think, Pitchfork was co-signing it. I think each and every one of us, as individual listeners and consumers of culture, has to come up with our own answer. I don't think there's a right or wrong answer. The thing that's interesting to me is that Pitchfork is a journalistic and critical organ. They do journalism and they do criticism. And then when they are making money to present an act—that's a co-sign, that's an endorsement. That's not just writing about and covering it. They very much wanted R. Kelly as their cornerstone artist for the festival. I think it's fair game to say: "Why, Pitchfork?"

I had purposely not listened to his music since the initial

charges came out, and I saw these ninth- and tenth-grade girls interviewed on TV, talking about how he was in the parking lot of their school every day and everyone knew how come. That is what it took for me.

Part of our reporting was sitting with those girls, sitting with their families, seeing their scars on their wrists, hearing the emotion.

Some of our young critical peers, they're 24 and all they know of Kelly's past is a vague idea of scandal; they were introduced to him as kids via _Space Jam._ A lot of your reporting on this is not online, it is not Googleable. Collective memory is that he "just" peed in a girl's mouth.

To be fair, I teach 20-year-olds at Columbia. Ignorance is nothing to be ashamed of. Nobody knows everything. A lot of art, great art, is made by despicable people. James Brown beat his wife. People are always, "Why aren't you upset about Led Zeppelin?" I got the Bonham three rings [tattooed] on my foot. Led Zeppelin did disgusting things. I read _Hammer of the Gods,_ I'm disgusted by the group sex with the shark. [Note: it was actually a red snapper! Still gross.] I have a couple of responses to that: I didn't cover Led Zeppelin. If I was on the plane, like Cameron Crowe was, I would have written about those things if I saw them.

The art very rarely talks about these things. There are not pro-rape Led Zeppelin songs. There are not pro-wife-beating James Brown songs. I think in the history of rock 'n' roll, rock music, or pop culture people misbehaving and behaving badly sexually with young women, rare is the amount of evidence compiled against anyone apart from R. Kelly. Dozens of girls—not one, not two, dozens—with harrowing lawsuits. The videotapes—and not just one videotape, numerous videotapes. And not Tommy Lee/Pam Anderson, Kardashian fun video. You watch the video for which he was indicted and there is the disembodied look of the rape victim. He orders her to call him Daddy. He urinates in her mouth and instructs her at great length on how to position herself to receive his "gift." It's a rape that you're watching. So we're not talking about rock star misbehavior, which men or women can do. We're talking about predatory behavior. Their lives were ruined. Read the lawsuits!

And there was a young woman who was pressured into an abortion?

That he paid for. There was a young woman that he picked up on the evening of her prom. The relationship lasted a year and a half or two years. Impregnated her, paid for her abortion, had his goons drive her. None of which she wanted. She sued him. The saddest fact I've learned is: Nobody matters less to our society than young black women. Nobody. They have any complaint about the way they are treated: They are "bitches, hoes, and gold-diggers," plain and simple. Kelly never misbehaved with a single white girl who sued him or that we know of. Mark Anthony Neal, the African-American scholar, makes this point: one white girl in Winnetka and the story would have been different.

No, it was young black girls and all of them settled. They settled because they felt they could get no justice whatsoever. They didn't have a chance.

And they learned that after putting these suits forth and having them get nowhere? Do you think they didn't get traction because of the representation they had, or Kelly's power? Were certain elements in concert with that?

I think it was a lot of things, including the fact that Kelly was fully capable of intimidating people. These girls feared for their lives. They feared for the safety of their families. And these people talked to me not because I'm super reporter—we rang a lot of doorbells on the South and West sides, and people were eager to talk about this guy, because they wanted him to stop!

Going back a little bit to our original question: You get this tape dropped in the mail...

Well, the tape came a year after we ran the first story. We ran this story and the world shrugged. Associated Press picks it up: "*Chicago Sun-Times* has reported a pattern of sexual predation of young women by Robert Kelly," and everybody says, "Ah, well, OK." Then one day I get this call that says: "Go to your mailbox. There's this manila envelope with a videotape in it."

We had gotten one videotape already after the first story, and we gave it to the police. When I say "we," I mean a roomful of editors sitting around asking, "What is the right thing to do here? This would seem to be evidence of a felony, we should give it to police." There was one tape, but the police could not determine the girl's age. The forensic experts they had looking at it said judging by the soles of her feet, they could tell she was 13 or 14 at the time this tape was made, but we can't identify who the woman is. Videotape No. 1.

There were tapes on the street. And I had heard of another video tape with a girl who was part of an ongoing relationship. This is the girl who was in the tape that was in the lawsuit.

And some 40 people testified that it was her?

Yeah. Coaches, best friend's parents, pastor, half the family, grandmother, aunt—but the mother and father never testified, the girl never testified. When we wrote our story about the tape, the girl and mother and father took a six-month vacation to the south of France. We'd been to the house several times. We'd rung the doorbell. This was an aluminum-siding, lower-middle-class house on the South Side, with a station wagon which is 13 years old—you know what I mean? And now they're in the south of France. And one time the dad got a credit as a bass player on an R. Kelly album. He didn't play bass.

The situations are incredibly complicated, and sometimes there is an element of, "We're gonna exploit this situation for our favor." That doesn't mean that it's legal or it's right or that girl wasn't harmed. It tore that family apart.

How many people do you think you've interviewed? How many people came forward?

I think in the end there were two dozen women with various level of details. Obviously the women who were part of the hundreds of pages of lawsuits—hell of a lot of details. There were girls who just told one simple story, and there were a lot of girls who told stories that lasted hours which still make me sick to my stomach. It never was one girl on one tape. Or one girl and Aaliyah.

The other thing, the thing that people seem to not know: She was fresh out of eighth grade in this tape.

Fourteen or 15. That puts a perspective on it. She's not sophisticated enough to know what her kinks are.

Let's talk about what it is, aside from not just having reportorial chops, that might hold somebody back. I feel that a lot of younger journalists came up through blogs, not journalism school. They are fearful to write about it because they don't know what they can say, what language they can use, if they can be sued for even acknowledging charges.

You may not know how to report, but you should know how to read. The *Sun-Times* was never sued for the hundreds of thousands of words that it wrote about R. Kelly. You cannot be sued for repeating anything that is in a lawsuit. You cannot be sued for repeating anything that was said during the six- or seven-week trial. It's in his record, and then there's Kelly's own words. Then read [Kelly's biography] *Soulacoaster*. It was not a pleasant experience for me to read *Soulacoaster*! But read it, and read what he says in his own book! Do your goddamn homework!

What are the other factors?

Here's the most sinister. This deeply troubles me: There's a very—I don't know what the percentage is—some percentage of fans are liking Kelly's music because they know. And that's really troublesome to me. There is some sort of—and this is tied up to complicated questions of racism and sexism—there is some sort of vicarious thrill to seeing this guy play this character in these songs and knowing that it's not just a character.

Songs like "Sexasaurus" make it novel. The ironic, jokey *Trapped in the Closet* series airs on the Independent Film Channel and features Will Oldham—that has these other hallmarks of "art" that read to a white, hipster, indie-rock audience.

It puts it in the realm of camp or kitsch. If you have an emotional reaction to a work of art and you use all your skills as a critic to back it up with evidence and context, that's all we can ask of anybody. We're all viewing art differently. The joy is in the conversation. Pitchfork is the premier critical organ in the United States for smart discussion of music, books, and artists, but it doesn't have this discussion. The site reviews his records but doesn't have the conversation about, "What does it say for us to like his music?"

I think, again, everybody has to individually answer. I can still listen to Led Zeppelin and take joy in Led Zeppelin or James Brown. I condemn the things they did. I'm not reminded constantly in the art, because the art is not about it. But if you're listening to "I want to marry you, pussy," and not realizing that he said that to Aaliyah, who was 14, and making an album he named *Age Ain't Nothing but a Number*—I had Aaliyah's mother cry on my shoulder and say her daughter's life was ruined, Aaliyah's life was never the same after that. That's not an experience you've had. I'm not expecting you to feel the same way I do. But you can look at this body of evidence. "You" meaning everybody who cares.

You told me about the night after your critical review of R. Kelly's performance at Pitchfork ran, one of these women called you at 2 a.m.

This happens a lot. If you are a good reporter, you are accessible to people and you cannot turn a story off. And that sucks! The number of times since I began this R. Kelly story that I was called in the middle of the night, was talking to someone on Christmas Eve or on New Year's Day or Thanksgiving... Yeah, I got a call from one of the women after the Pitchfork Festival review. "I know we haven't spoken in a long time," and said thank you for still caring and thank you for writing this story, because nobody gives a shit.

It was a horrible day and a horrible couple of weeks when he was acquitted. The women I heard from who I'd interviewed, women I'd never interviewed who said, "I didn't come forward, I never spoke to you before, I wish I had now that son of a bitch got off." Jesus Christ. Rape-victim advocates—I don't believe in god—they do God's work. These young women who volunteer to be in the emergency room and sit with a woman throughout the horrible process, I don't do that. I'm not saying I'm even in the same universe. But somebody calls you up and says I want to talk about this, or thank you about writing this, or, "I can't sleep because I'm haunted, can you hear what I want to tell you?" We do that as a human being. I would like to forget about this story. I'm not saying I'm super reporter. I'm saying this was a huge story. Where was everybody else?

There is a disregard for your ongoing concern about this. "Let this go, Jim. Get over it, Jim. He was acquitted." You have never dropped this, and your peers are pissed because it puts the rest of us over a barrel. I can speak to this, too. It's often uncool to be the person who gives a shit.

"You're jealous of R. Kelly, you're trying to make your name off his career."

Because you would love nothing more than to have to report and carry these stories of sexual assault.

It is on record. In the dozens. So stop hedging your words, and when you tell me what a brilliant ode to pussy *Black Panties* is, then realize that the next sentence should say: "This, from a man who has committed numerous rapes." The guy was a monster! Just say it! We do have a justice system and he was acquitted. OK, fine. And these other women took the civil lawsuit route. He was tried on very narrow grounds. He was tried on a 29-minute, 36-second videotape. He was tried on trading child pornography. He was not tried for rape. He was acquitted of making child pornography. He's never been tried in court for rape, but look at the statistics. The numbers of rapes that happened, the numbers of rapes that were reported, the numbers of rapes that make it to court and then the conviction rate.

I mean, it comes down to something minuscule. He's never had his day in court as a rapist. It's 15 years in the past now, but this record exists. You have to make a choice, as a listener, if music matters to you as more than mere entertainment. And you and I have spent our entire lives with that conviction. This is not just entertainment, this is our lifeblood. This matters.

PART
TWO

REAL/FAKE

GAGA TAKES A TRIP

Nashville Scene, **April 2011**

There's this photo. In it, Lady Gaga is framed tight, center of the picture, shot from far away by staked-out paparazzi, perhaps hiding out behind a row of chairs or a ficus. There are blurred objects around the edges, and there are frames within the frames—distant glass security cordons. The dark, lumpy figure of a TSA agent looms to the left, hands near the star, extended rigidly, officially. Lady Gaga does not acknowledge the camera: She is not looking at it, but there is no part of her presentation that does not anticipate the camera's gaze, and subsequently, ours as well.

Lady Gaga is taking a trip and has arrived at Los Angeles International Airport in full pop regalia. She is not like the other blond pop singers—Madonna or Jessica Simpson—who deplane in comfort sweats, their makeup-free faces looking strangely unfamiliar, a ponytail sticking out from their ball cap. Gaga does not dress like she is headed home from a yoga workshop even when flying across the continent. Gaga teases out the fan fantasy of the pop star by never dropping the act—she's like a superhero, never appearing out of uniform. She never snaps us back to reality; we stay with her in the weird, glamorous world she has made real.

In this, she is conceding the duality of pop stardom: this is all surface and finessed-to-please presentation, an impossible manufacture. She one-ups all those who decry her work and platinum pop as not "real" music—because it's all "fake"—by making it *the most fabulous fake that ever faking faked*. To be sure, Gaga's "fake" is at least as real as the "real" of any self-conscious Brooklyn beardo 'bout to be discovered by Pitchfork.

Here, amid her TSA-administered security screening, Gaga is looking spectacular—as in, like a spectacle, which is how we want her to be—and she is not disappointing. She is wearing perilously-tall (10-inch) Alexander McQueen snakeskin platform heels, which the designer is said to have modeled after an armadillo. Their fronts arch from the ankle in a smooth half moon that is blunted by the floor, like a toucan's bill if it pointed down instead of out. They are leathery and gleam in the light, and they look unlike shoes anyone's ever seen. Their protrusion is strange, but there is something natural to the line—it's easy to think them as hooves. Gaga's legs are covered only by what appears to be industrial-strength fishnet pantyhose that go up under her shiny black belt. Looped through the right front of the belt is a pair of metal handcuffs. Her flowing white wig cascades down to her stomach, she wears round, Lennon-style sunglasses, there is a phone in her hand. Most of her outfit is accessories, the only clothing she has on is a pair of "nude" bikini underwear and a bra, and a golden jacket, of which she is wearing only one sleeve, with the other half seemingly tucked into her back waistband—a curious slip of modesty to cover one's ass while appearing nearly naked in public.

In this picture, we see Gaga as White Swan to out-of-control Britney Spears' Black Swan. This outfit is similar to the one worn by Spears in summer of 2008, in one of the bleaker paparazzi shots taken during her lost years. A pale, blemished Spears is shown clad in ripped black fishnets, black cowboy boots, a black jacket, mini skirt hiked up her waist, revealing her blood-stained underwear. She wears oversized black sunglasses, and her hair is dyed black—her weave a ratted mess—and there is a phone in her hand. She is heading in to L.A. boutique Kitson for a private shopping spree at 2 a.m.

Though Gaga's work is as platinum-perfect (perhaps even more so) as Britney's, Gaga's work is rife with irony and self-possession—she satisfies with a cultivated, purposeful strangeness. She should by all means be the Black Swan of the two, and as she plays with the idea of pop's manufacture, she winks at us from atop her skyscraper heels. Being nearly nude in LAX, she obliges our most debased wish: to see celebrities naked, to ogle them, completely. She acknowledges the ironies, the ruptures, the fantasies of pop, and she abides by them as she rips them apart. In doing so, Lady Gaga shows that she understands the only real rule of popular entertainment: Give the people what they want.

DECONSTRUCTING LANA DEL REY

SPIN magazine, January 2012

I. The Origin Story: A Star Is Born/Made

The myth, as it is presently understood: Lana Del Rey is a vanity project bankrolled by the singer's dad and honed, over the years, by a series of lawyers and managers who've shaped her image and plotted her career path. She is a canvas of a girl and a willing one at that. Her real name is Lizzy Grant, "Lana Del Rey" is "fake," as are her lips.

What we do know to be true: Lizzy Grant is indeed now Lana Del Rey. She is 25 and grew up in Lake Placid, in upstate New York. "I lived in a small town," she told MTV, "and I just thought it was gonna be a long life." She spent her time as a teen wandering in the woods and writing, feeling like a secret weirdo and having her first real connection to music through Biggie's "Juicy." Back then, she says she was something akin to trouble, and got shipped off to Kent, a private prep school in Connecticut. Her autobiography of that era can be heard on the track "This Is What Makes Us Girls."

At 18, she moved to New York to attend Fordham University, where she studied metaphysics, looking for proof of God, and began writing songs. She stopped drinking and got sober. She played shows, performing versions of songs that now make up *Born to Die*. Just before her senior year, she found a deal with the small independent label 5 Points, through a songwriting competition. The label gave her an advance, which she used to move into a trailer park in New Jersey shortly after graduating from Fordham.

David Nichtern, who runs 5 Points, solicited producer David Kahne (who has worked with everyone from Paul McCartney to Sublime), who agreed to helm the Lizzy Grant record. "It was a bit of a coup because he is a big name, and we are a tiny record label," says Nichtern. In the studio, Kahne saw in Del Rey a singer who was motivated and self-directed, always looking for ways to move her work forward. "What she's doing goes against the grain of chart pop," says Kahne. "The country is fraying at the edges; she wanted to look at that edge, at destruction and loss, and talk about it." According to

Kahne, Del Rey was "solitary" and often spent her nights riding the subway out to Coney Island, exploring.

The songs from these sessions were split into two releases, the *Kill Kill* EP and her debut album. According to Nichtern, after the release of the EP, the singer said she wanted to change the name she recorded under. "First it was 'Del R-A-Y,' and then she settled on 'R-E-Y.' This story that it was anyone but her making the decision is complete fiction," says Nichtern. "If she is 'made up'—well, she is the one who made herself up. She has very strong ideas about what she does. The idea someone could manage her into a particular shape—it's impossible."

Shortly before the full-length was to be released, Nichtern says Del Rey decided she was unhappy and wanted to add tracks amongst other changes. "It became difficult to go forward," he explains. Del Rey decided to shelve the record, and 5 Points obliged, striking a deal for her to buy back her masters. Nichtern is adamant that the deal's dissolution was all aboveboard and there were never any hard feelings. "She is a great artist," he says, "a real artist. I have always thought so and still do."

"It was very unusual," says Interscope's Executive VP of A&R Larry Jackson of his first serious meeting with Lana Del Rey. "We sat for an hour and talked, without her playing any of her music. Just conversation, honing in on the philosophy of what she was doing, what she saw for herself. It was a totally unorthodox meeting, and I thought, 'I've got to do this.'" When asked if anyone else was involved, if there is someone orchestrating Lana from behind the curtain, Jackson is emphatic. "The only Svengali in this thing is Lana."

"I've never understood this controversy about whether she is real or fake," says rapper/producer Princess Superstar. "All artists have a persona." A year prior to the Interscope deal, the two women spent a few months honing Del Rey's songs, with the rapper serving as mentor. "She's not put together by some company. These are her songs, her melodies, her singing—she's always had this '60s aesthetic. Look at Katy Perry and Beyoncé, and you see that they have a team."

Interscope don Jimmy Iovine gave Jackson his blessing to sign Del Rey on the basis of seeing an unfinished version of "Video Games" on YouTube. Del Rey signed a worldwide, joint deal with Interscope and Polydor in March 2011, making her, officially, a major-label recording artist a full six months before anyone was pondering whether the former choirgirl was a plasticine creation.

II. The Look: Baddest of the Good Girls

A pretty singer with a cool voice is one thing, but Lana Del Rey fascinates because of the tension in her persona. She's the good girl who wants it all—the boy, his heart, and nothing short of pop stardom, even if that ambition ends up making you look pretty ugly. In short, Lana Del Rey is Amy Winehouse with the safety on. While Winehouse was unrepentantly bad, Del Rey plays it differently—she's a bad girl who knows better, the bad girl being held back within the good girl. Her ballads are about self-control (or sometimes lack of it) and being hopelessly dedicated to bird-dogging dudes ("You're no good for me / But, baby, I want you" goes Del Rey's "Diet Mountain Dew"). The Lana of "Blue Jeans" and "Video Games" is charmed by the darkness, thrilled by the prospect of losing herself in this bad boy, finding form in his needs. The Lana of these songs is alive in that vicarious freedom—evidence that there's still some teenage-crazy, ride-or-die bitch lingering around her Chantilly edges. "I've had to pray a lot because I've been in trouble a lot," she told *GQ* last year.

"I remember that she had really specific feelings about what she wanted to portray about girls," recalls Kahne. "We were talking about Marilyn and Natalie Wood, these iconic actresses of the '50s, and she said, 'They were good girls.' She liked that image."

"In her, I do see the struggle between the good girl and the bad girl," says Larry Jackson. That duality was part of what made him want to sign her. After a dinner meeting in Los Angeles last spring, he saw her kick a cab that cut her off as she was walking away. "She cursed out the cab. I saw her do it, but she didn't see me. She epitomizes the loose-cannon star."

In a YouTube video from 2008, back when she was still firmly in Lizzy Grant mode, Del Rey gives a writer from *Index* magazine a tour of her New Jersey trailer park. Gracious and proud, she smiles easily. It's a year after Winehouse's "Rehab" hit ubiquity, and Del

Rey is done up in a Jersey approximation of the singer: She's wearing a silk bomber, her white blonde flip teased to a bouffant puff and tied up with a bandana do-rag, batting long fake lashes. She looks miscast—like a too-young housewife—a child bride trying to look grown. Her baby face and coquettish giggle give her away. The sound on the video is awful and the questions tepid, but Del Rey answers the two most important ones clearly and directly to the camera: This is where she wrote her record; and she moved to Jersey for the state's surplus of metal boys. There is no mistaking what matters to her.

"She has many different qualities that women in our culture aren't allowed to be, all at once, so people are trying to find the inauthentic one," says Tavi Gevinson, the founding editor of teen-girl mag *Rookie*. "She's girly, but not infantilized. I relate to her aesthetic the way I think other girls relate to Taylor Swift lyrics—her femininity isn't too sexy or too pure, and that's something I can get behind."

How Del Rey defines herself in the classic-pop cosmos has changed as her music and image have evolved over the past year: "Gangsta Nancy Sinatra" gave way to the slightly more finessed "Lolita lost in the 'hood." More recently, she catchphrased her major label debut *Born to Die* as "Bruce Springsteen in Miami," trading up on that Jersey striving. *Born to Die* features familiar Springsteen tropes—no-future kids tangled in sin and forever promises; Del Rey's songs are like answer-back dispatches direct from "Candy's Room," but the door's slammed shut and the stereo's up. She's telling the missing side of the story, revealing a new, true character living behind that scrim of male desire: *Born To Die* is the good girl who wants it just as bad as he does.

III. The Backlash: It's About the Music, LOL

The issue with Lana Del Rey is not whether she is a corporate test-tubed ingénue, but why we are unwilling to believe that she is animated by her own passion and ambition—and why that makes a hot girl so unattractive. The big question here is not "Is she real?" But, rather, why it seems impossible to believe that she could be.

On its surface, the Lana Del Rey Authenticity Debate™ swings between two depressing possibilities: (1) That's she's all but the fourth

Kardashian sister, Frankensteined together (by old white guys) in order to exploit the now sizable "indie" market, or (2) that she is a moderately-talented singer who is getting over by pushing our buttons with nostalgia and good looks. This is the distracting crux, a pointless debate that casts a long shadow over *Born to Die*. For critics and anonymous commenters alike, the reality of Lana Del Rey seems to be an unsolvable equation: the prospect of an attractive female artist who sings plainly about her desire because she has it, with an earnest vision, who crafts her own songs and videos, who understands what it takes to be a viable pop product and is capable of guiding herself to those perilous heights. It's seemingly beyond possibility. Yet, Lana Del Rey is doing it all, before our very eyes.

Being sexy and serious about your art needn't be mutually exclusive, even when your art involves being a pop package. Defending herself to *Pitchfork* last fall, Del Rey said, "I'm not trying to create an image or a persona. I'm just singing because that's what I know how to do." If her ambitions were to "just" sing, she'd still be making the rounds at Brooklyn open mics—but here she's attempting to refocus our attention on her music. Which, for a short time, was the reason we cared about her. Perhaps, if she'd faked us out with a record on a modest indie label like Merge first, some hesitation towards major labels or the mainstream, all her ambition would've been palatable instead of outrageous.

The central, mistaken assumption being made about Del Rey is that she is a valence for DIY/indie culture, which she's never been. She played daytime, industry showcases at overlit venues in Midtown for years, and was taking meetings at majors since mid-2010. These are the steps of someone who wants to be a pop star, not signed by Matador. Bloggers and tastemaking websites believed they noticed her first, when, in fact, they were two years behind a pack of lawyers and A&R scouts who were eager to sign an artist who was the total package.

While a few (two) blogs got on the Del Rey wagon early—successive waves of attention in late spring of 2011 were prompted by press releases. No one rightly discovered her and even the coolest blogs were being jumped into by publicists or "grassroots" marketing firms, their LDR posts repeating the story as it was fed to them. Many of these same blogs are now indignant, fronting like they were duped into caring about her or lending her credibility—though they certainly weren't so discerning before. They were just eager to claim "first," as is the law of the jungle.

In the weeks surrounding the release of Del Rey's *Born to Die*, every interview and TV performance became a new proving ground. Video interviews showed Del Rey as both self-aware and funny, as when a VH1 interviewer condescendingly comforted her for not being on this year's Coachella lineup. She deadpanned, "Aw, thanks," before cracking herself up. Her much-maligned Saturday Night Live performance sounded just as awkward as every other band that performs on the show. Still, her unevenness was taken as resounding proof that she was Born 2 Fail by no less an authority than NBC news anchor Brian Williams.

In other interviews, Del Rey has talked about studying cosmology and a six-year stint doing homeless outreach, suggesting that she's more engaged in the real word than her ardent critics. Though she aims high, she's still hardly acting like a star, telling MTV, "I consider being able to pursue music a luxury, but it's not the most important thing in my life. It's just something that's really nice that ended up working for me for right now." Still, she doesn't bother hiding her ambition—she's cited the self-actualization classic *Think and Grow Rich* as her recommended reading.

Surprisingly, it's still easier for people to believe the ancient model of a major-label star system—girl of moderate talent is groomed and posed to appeal—rather than accept that a young woman could plot her course by her own animus. Meanwhile, sexist critiques of Del Rey's appearance, songs and videos get spun as incisive discernment, offered up as knowing analysis of a deceptive product. Her songs are assailed as "trying too hard" to be sexy, as if we have slept through the past three decades of liberated pop-diva sexuality as written by Madonna/Janet/Britney/Rihanna and are now shocked by Del Rey's slight approximation. She's by-the-book, and yet she's seen as breaking the rules. It's doubtful we'd even be intrigued by a female artist being subtle or modest. As an audience, we make a big stink about wanting the truth, but we're only really interested in the old myths.

TAYLOR SWIFT, GRIMES AND LANA DEL REY: THE YEAR IN BLOND AMBITION

Village Voice **Pazz & Jop Critics Poll, January 2012**

It seems so long ago—certainly more than 52 weeks—since we were all flustered by the audacity of Lana Del Rey. Her crimes, it seemed, were legion and very, very serious—concerns that trumped consideration of whether or not her music was any good. She was bad on Saturday Night Live. Her lips, perhaps, had collagen in them. A few years ago, she was playing A&R showcases backed by hired guns, and suddenly she was all over *Pitchfork* like a real-deal indie ingénue, but (gasp!) it turned out she already had a deal with Interscope. Her name was not actually Lana Del Rey, and, unlike any artist in the history of ever, she'd attended private school.

As we enter the new year with a clean slate and hindsight, it seems fair enough to chalk up our lil' Lana freak-out to our long-standing weirdness with women's ambition and the antiquated notion that image consciousness is somehow antithetical to the making of true art and is, in fact, a sin against rock's visceral mandate. It's a problem we tend to have with girls and women more than with the boys (word to Jack White's continuing Campaign 4 Realness). This past year proved there is a special sort of animus reserved for women— Lana Del Rey, Taylor Swift and Grimes' Claire Boucher—whose ambition seems especially naked and, if you will, feminine.

It's only natural that young female artists engage us with and communicate through their image(s) as much as they do with their music. Image is a more effective vehicle for expression than songs. No girl escapes teenhood without a keen awareness of exactly how the world sees her, what it expects of her; she knows the weight of the world's desire for her down to the ounce.

When it comes to music, image is believed to be the teen girls' area of fascination and special expertise; young women's arduous fandom is often taken as the very proof of a performer's artlessness. The perception being that girls are so rapt with an artist's surface image that it supersedes any sort of real connection with or understanding of the music itself. Though Swift and Boucher placed high in this year's Pazz & Jop—Lana less so (*Born to Die*, #54 album)—the critique with all three has often regarded the seeming purposefulness of artifice in their image, as well as their dutiful maintenance of it.

We took Lana's ambitions personally—as if she was preying upon us, marking us as hornball simps so seduced by her porny licking of her fake/not-fake lips that we'd buy in on whatever it was she was selling. The offense being? That we'd actually fall for something so constructed? Or was it the fact of the construction itself?

Part of what made Boucher's work so exciting this year was her zealous courtship of the zeitgeist, the irreverence of her ambition, that her cultural reference points were young and female. She's an autodidactic indie artist who pinpoints the unnatural qualities of Mariah Carey's voice as her greatest influence. Subversion of manga imagery and lost-in-the-mix, baby-voiced cooing are far from the riot-grrrl-influenced rage that we commonly use to verify feminist artistry.

Boucher's merchandising of "pussy rings" was overtly feminist, though some still wrote it off as a ploy for attention. Boucher had the temerity to manufacture merch that wasn't a T-shirt—a feminist rebuttal to the cock-'n'-balls scrawled on every dressing room wall. How is a plastic rendering of a vulva so utterly *escandalo* in the Internet age of 2012? (The gender divide on the pussy-ring reporting is stark and telling of just how and who Grimes connects with.) While Boucher can be faulted for some things—is that a rain stick sample on "Know the Way?"—would she really be a more credible artist if she showed less ambition?

Swift, who is a little younger than Boucher and Del Rey, had a year of evolution for her image as well. On *Red*, Swift deflects power with a studied naiveté. Love is something that she falls victim to; men are fundamentally the bad actors. She's amid an incredibly careful transition from pop's Virgin Queen into young adulthood, so now it's slightly less of a big deal to *imply* that she has had a boy sleepover in a song. Swift is nothing if not a cautious star, a multimillion-dollar industry unto herself—she is not going to pull a Miley in order to signal what a big girl she is now. Throughout *Red*, she is frequently seduced, victimized or unable to steel herself against her own desires, as if adult womanhood is a powerful undertow dragging her out to the sea. It's a curious thing to watch such a powerful cultural force abdicate her own might, but it's understood that claiming it comes with its own cross.

Swift's mastery of her own feckless image is as finely-honed a piece of work as any of *Red*'s half-dozen singles; it engages many of the common expectations of girlhood, so much so that it presents us with an impossibly perfected persona. The controlled iterations of Swift are subject to constant remix due to her celebrity status, where her songs conflate with the tabloid fare of her life and create a larger, narrative work. Be they peer, cad or Kennedy, each new Swift boyfriend presents or disproves a song theorem of *Red*. In the latest widely circulated pap shot of Swift, she's exiting a tropical isle alone via small craft. It reads as forlorn from a distance of a pixelated 30 yards and adds chiaroscuro to "Sad Beautiful Tragic." Swift's got a Joni problem now: The interest in whom she's seeing and speculation over which song is about which dude now obfuscates the merits of her work (though it is hard to suggest any human force could blunt the thundering Max Martin'd chorus of "Trouble," but alas).

To be galled by these women's advances upon their audiences is to play the Pollyanna about how any product gets across the transom to us. In their manipulations and fluid manifestations of their images, they each show incredible deftness—a cultural prescience that speaks to their ambition and interest in being understood. All this girlish guile makes their art no less pure.

WE CAN'T STOP: OUR YEAR WITH MILEY

Village Voice **Pazz & Jop Critics Poll, January 2014**

Is there a scribe among us—save for *Wire* writers and those whose bylines eagerly accompanied reviews of that Larry Coryell reissue—who didn't pull down at least $40 for Miley musings in 2013? Perhaps a shocked-and-awed news item, a post-VMAs reaction, a pondering of that preponderance of tongue? If not, I hate to break it to you, but you got ripped off. It was her year, whether we liked it or—well, yeah.

We wrote about Miley perhaps not so much because she fascinated but riled us with her every move. And to be sure, it was the moves—of her masturbatory fingers, nude body, her twerking, her waggling tongue, the way she used other women's bodies and her own in videos and performances. Her actual album, *Bangerz*, was a tertiary concern at best.

It was a long year for pop aggrievement; exempting Bruno Mars' five-week run at the top of the year, the No. 1 spot on *Billboard* in 2013 was occupied by white artists. While those Baauer, Macklemore, Robin Thicke, and Lorde hits got their share of controversy and think-piece lather, nothing disquieted us as thoroughly as Miley. She did a mere three weeks with "Wrecking Ball," but spent the last half of the year as a lightning rod for our censure and outrage; we cut off her head and she just kept writhing, unchastened.

Writing about Miley is simple because she's impossible to define and easy to vilify—whatever we want to billboard onto her sticks because all at once she is enrapturing, repulsive, hysterical, ignorant, white, young, female, ultra-rich, sexy, scary, skeezy, unafraid, feminist, an artist, not feminist, privileged, talented, sad, visceral, fake, real, too real, and friends with Terry Richardson. What *can't* we say about her? Apparently nothing. Bad girls are infinite. Miley possesses us in a way that fully clothed Lorde never will.

Yet the sins of Miley were real. She made egregious missteps amid her attempts to telegraph her artistic primacy, appropriating black cultural idioms and playing on historically racist stereotypes. She claimed she doesn't see or consider race, and of course she doesn't have to *consider* race—she's a very rich and successful white woman living in America. To ask her to see the scope of her privilege—to understand what it means to mean-mug and then push in her gleaming grill, to really get how a swipe of her tongue across Amazon Ashley's ass could play to anyone but herself—is an act of futility. Miley's defensive assertion that we were all prudes with a problem illustrated how wide the chasm between her actions and her awareness was. It made her naiveté seem willful, emblematic—it made her continual triumph downright enraging.

Then there's the matter of the paucity of imagination in how Miley served herself to us in 2013, permanently lensed in the pornographic gaze. Every glance was a demand to imagine what it is to fuck her or to imagine ourselves as her, being consumed. By the time the video for "Adore You" was released in December, Miley's pussy-as-Thor's-hammer pretext and uncomplicated invitations began to feel ruthless in their continual deploy. Their cheap power was fatiguing.

If there was any discernible deep thought behind the image, *Bangerz* could have been a masterful Top 40 long con, a work of weapons-grade performance art on par with, say, Valie Export's Actionist peepshow *Action Pants: Genital Panic*. Miley engaged our baseness and biases, only to make us confront how much we want to see, how much we've been culturally sensitized to be turned on by a rich, white bitch daring us to want her, watching us as we watch her. By year's end, she'd utterly failed to shock anyone who was still paying attention. Which, if we're being honest, was all of us.

In the same week "Adore You" dropped, Miley offered up a hopeful revision of herself to *The New York Times*. If taken at face value, it would seem we've misunderstood her all along: She's a Mandela-mourning, big-tent feminist living in hope for America's post-racial future. She doesn't want to be a bad example to the youth, but she's got a rebel nature. She claims she respected her Disney-branding enough to curtail it till she was legal. The part of that complex equation that actually jibes with the Miley we recognize is that *yoke of Disney*. Her grown-up image requires a constant reminder of her Disnified past to show us just how wayward we should understand Miley to be. They made millions branding Miley as a clean-fun-loving, purity-ring-clasping everygirl; Disney had her formally apologize for taking bikini selfies after the then-teenage singer's phone was hacked and pics disseminated. It is only natural that even the most tepid, predictable adulteration of Miley's emblematically pure image would be sensational, that it would have the power to horrify us.

Miley's *Bangerz*-era story is a transformation fantasy built on proximity to what she was, how we knew her, how fast she went from supersweet to superfreak, suggesting that, yes, she was an authentic bad girl all along under that darling disguise. Her drifting orientation from the Mouse mothership is meant to tell us as much about who she is now as when she cried real tears and writhed nude on a wrecking ball for Richardson's camera. This is her ceremony to show us, whether we want her or not, she belongs to us now.

LOUDER THAN LOVE:
MY TEEN GRUNGE POSERDOM
EMP Conference paper, Spring 2005

There was a time, not too terribly long ago, when I was not cool. In 1990, I was 14, almost 15, and just entered the ninth grade at the largest high school in Minneapolis and was orbiting somewhere between loner dork and amorphous weirdo. My wardrobe consisted of a lot of black clothes, a lot of orange clothes, my mother's business apparel from the '80s; I wore cowboy boots and long, unbelted tunics that made me look like I was in a cult. I spent a lot of time alone, sewing hats and reading news magazines to keep up on international politics. The music I knew about was from the radio. I had a few tapes I liked: the B-52's *Cosmic Thing*, Deee-Lite, the first Tracy Chapman album. I mostly listened to the tapes on the weekend, when I was delivering my newspaper route, though sometimes I would lay in bed at night and listen to the Tracy Chapman tape over and over and cry a little.

Six weeks after I started high school, I was sitting on the bleachers during freshman gym class, which I was already failing for refusing to dress for class, along with all the other weirdos, who were also refusing gym on principle. Andrew Semans, also of the ninth grade, came and sat next to me and asked, "Are you a punk or a hippie? I can't tell." I told him I liked The Clash, and he started drilling me about a million bands I had never heard. The next day he handed me a cassette tape, a mix made from a very specific subsection of his big brother's record collection. Butthole Surfers, Babes in Toyland, Boredoms, BALL, Big Black, Bongwater on side one; Pussy Galore, Voidoids, Stooges on the flip. By week's end I was a convert and punk-identified.

As punk rock began to ravage and motivate my life, so did my adolescent hormones. I began to pine for for the attention of punk boys, of which I knew three. One of which was Andrew and we could barely stand one another but were bonded by conversations about Sonic Youth. His friend Ted who wore a Jane's Addiction T-shirt and was on JV bowling; he thought *All Shook Down* was the best Replacements record—making him a no go. Then there was Andrew

Beccone, who was in the tenth grade, who wasn't so much punk as he was proactively grunge.

He became my crush by default, by virtue of the fact that he knew my name and he knew who Hüsker Dü was, and at the time that was more than I had going with anyone else. His look was proto grunge, he wore his hair long and in a middle part, all his jeans were ripped, he wore a faded Mudhoney *Superfuzz Bigmuff* T-shirt and a flannel. He played drums in a cover band of sorts with his college-age brother; they were called Korova Milkbar and their only gigs were in their basement. Their repertoire read like a best-of Sub Pop sampler: Tad's "Loser," Nirvana's "Lovebuzz" and "Floyd the Barber," a Soundgarden song, a Screaming Trees song, and they usually closed their set with a Mudhoney medley that included an infinite version of "In 'n' Out of Grace" that would alternate between the chorus and long drum solos. Because I "loved" Andrew and wanted him to love me back, and though I was approximately 4 feet tall, had a mouth full of braces and looked as much like a 14-year-old boy as I did a 14-year-old girl, I took the only route available—I became a grunge devotee.

The process was simple: I made the rounds to every record store in the Twin Cities, spending my hard-earned babysitting and paper-delivery savings on anything with a Sub Pop logo on it, every release in multiple formats—Mudhoney, Nirvana, Fluid, Tad, Dwarves, Soundgarden, L7 and Dickless. I saved up $100 for the out-of-print *Sub Pop 100* compilation. I mail-ordered five Mudhoney, two Fluid, and one Soundgarden shirt and then made my own Nirvana shirt with a Sharpie.

I parted my hair in the middle, ripped holes in the knees of my jeans, scrawled the names of every band I liked on my Chuck Taylor high-tops in pen. I am not sure why I thought dressing *exactly* like Andrew Beccone might lure him to me, but I wanted to show him we were kindred spirits in the world, toughing out our teenage times with Tad's *8-Way Santa* in our Walkmans.

Alas, the pose did not end there. I did things like casually wander past his classes as they got out, holding nothing but a Mudhoney tape in my hand, as if that was the only supply one needed for ninth grade. I took the same Russian class as him so that I would have the chance to tell him such things as I was considering getting a tattoo of Mudhoney bassist Matt Lukin, "once I got the money together." My project for film class was a documentary on his band, and it was 20 minutes of carefully edited footage of band practices in his parents' basement, and nothing but (I got a C-). I went to see Fluid twice that year, despite hating them, in hopes of seeing him at the show. When I saw him that following Monday, as I was artfully lingering outside his AP English class, I said "I figured I would have seen you at the show last night," he told me he was *no longer into Fluid*. I was crushed. I had spent dozens of hours listening to their records—which I found to be unbearable—fantasizing and prepping for conversations about Fluid minutiae that we would one day have.

All soul soon left my pose. My obsession with detail slipped. I was coming to the agonizing conclusion that all of this, my teen-girl masking, was in vain. I'd dedicated several months and several hundred dollars on trying to cultivate a connection that was never going to be. Still, I wasn't quite ready to give up the masquerade.

At the end of the school year, I managed to get invited to a party where all three of the school's grunge cover bands were playing. I would soon have the chance to see my crush-object one last time before the span of summer. I went to the party wearing a Soundgarden *Louder Than Love* T-shirt, which I had purchased for the occasion. I slouched up against a wall, peacocking my ennui, sipping a Miller Lite and pretending to be way into that, too. I was standing next to Andrew's best friend, Mike, who was setting up a bass rig. I ventured to ask him what was this awesome record we were listening to? He gawked at me, appalled, "Uh? *Louder Than Love*?" I scrambled, mortified, and insisted I was too wasted to recognize Soundgarden, the most distinctive band of the grunge genre.

I then had the torturous experience of then watching Mike walk over to Andrew and relay this anecdote and then Andrew look towards me and snicker. I left the party, walked home and cried myself to sleep.

Less than a month later, I picked up a compilation called *Kill Rock Stars*. While my purchase was initially fueled by the inclusion of Nirvana and Melvins tracks, both potential conversation topics with Andrew, but something entirely different happened when

I heard a band on side A, Bikini Kill. Kathleen Hanna's rebel yell posted the bail from my teen grunge prison; I had found music that meant everything to *me*. The band's *Bikini Kill* fanzine and the cassette demo meant I no longer had a reason to be obsessing over music that *meant nothing*. I was liberated from my days spent walking past some boy's locker, loudly humming Nirvana songs. Bikini Kill songs taught me something that neither Mudhoney, nor Andrew Beccone ever could—that my teen-girl soul mattered. That who I was mattered, what I thought and felt mattered, even when they were invisible to everyone else.

PART
THREE

NOSTALGIA

WHEN THE BOSS WENT MORAL: BRUCE SPRINGSTEEN'S LOST ALBUM

The American Prospect, **November 2010**

What is pop music for if not escape? It lifts us out of our everyday, our workday, to stoke and coalesce our fantasies about romance or an alternate life, away from where we've detoured. In 1977, Bruce Springsteen began recording the album that would become the landmark *Darkness on the Edge of Town*, and it was that escapist idea of pop that he was working with. Informed by Elvis, Orbison and Brill Building songwriters, he was penning from that tradition: grand, lovelorn tunes of cars and girls and memories that were easy to relate to. Springsteen was eager to prove himself more than a one-hit wonder off the popularity of *Born To Run* and feeling the schism between where his new success placed him and the blue-collar caste from which he rose. This schism is very much the place that pop is meant to offer escape from—and it's what began to drive and shape *Darkness*. Springsteen wanted to speak from that unresolvable place, to confine the listener in that underclass discomfort.

Those tracks that didn't fit that vision now make up *The Promise*—a lost album of sorts. These 22 tracks are immaculate—a glut of fine work from The Boss at the dawn of his prime. Some of the tracks here reappear in slightly different forms on *Darkness* and later albums ("Candy's Boy," "Racing in the Street ('78)," the opening refrain of "Spanish Eyes" would later appear in "I'm On Fire"). It's easy to hear that some of these could have been hits for Springsteen—and wonder why they're absent from *Darkness*. As an album, *Darkness* is lean and ready, marks of the influence of Springsteen's recent conversion to both punk rock and Hank Williams; many of these tracks are ballads and polished anthems with large debts to the formalist sensibilities of Spector, Lieber and Stoller, King and Goff. More than their sound, what kept these cuts off *Darkness* is that the story that Springsteen wanted to tell was a moral one.

Darkness was an attempt to ask impossibly big questions about life and liberty in America, what it meant to be a man, the meaning of work in a capitalist system, and, as Springsteen explained later, how to deal with sin in a good life. He spent five months in the studio with the E Street Band working out the hungry ghosts of his Catholic boyhood, until he found a way contain them in *Darkness'* anxious blaze. He refused the gleaming pop tracks and lovelorn balladry that make up *The Promise*—turning "Because the Night" over to Patti Smith because he *knew* it was a hit, a song that would define him, and he wasn't interested in that.

Whether Springsteen was seeking to become rock's beleaguered blue-collar conscience or he just wanted to be more than a standard-issue rock star is debatable, but it's safe to assume that one doesn't endeavor to spend years laboring over the allegorical language with which to best illuminate the spiritual longing of the American underclass if you aren't fully convinced of your own powers. Whether Springsteen was interested in being rock's great moralist is beside the point—*Darkness* is what earned him the job.

Listening to *The Promise* it's easy to understand that if any of these tracks would have made it onto *Darkness* it would changed the record's entire character. These are songs about kisses ("Fire," "The Little Things"), 14 of them are about his feelings for a girl. All this lovin' and radio-listenin' and car-buildin' on *The Promise* doesn't emotionally square with a *Darkness* track like "Adam Raised a Cain"—a song about shouldering the legacy you inherit from your parents—or the album's reckoning, "The Promised Land." Even as desperate as "Because the Night" is—with Springsteen sounding so plaintive and vulnerable—it would have worked against the macho confidence he exudes on "Candy's Room." "The Promise" chronicles disenfranchisement from the American Dream and could have fit, but its bathos would have undercut the hope that is *Darkness'* covenant with the listener.

While *The Promise* comes as a standalone double disc, it's perhaps better to take it in its other form, sandwiched within the context of the *Darkness on the Edge of Town* box set; a reproduction of Springsteen's notebook from the sessions, three CDs (*The Promise* and *Darkness*) and three DVDs, including a making-of *Darkness* DVD that is culled from archival footage from rehearsals and sessions and a phenomenal vintage concert performance. Seeing the scope of Springsteen's bright-eyed intent and his commitment, to *Darkness'* message, to his music, to his talent and his fans—believing in the power of music to communicate something so complex—makes the man seem heroic. By aiming to make such moral music, he made a new mimetic mold. Here we have the complete package, of all that you'd really want your rock stars to be—the longing loverman, the prove-it-all-night rock star, and the regular guy staking his guts to the stage, the craftsman capable of putting all your too-familiar restlessness into a song you'd wanna hear a thousand times.

The album's emotional truth mirrors its political one. The Carter-era malaise to which *Darkness* was born is palpable. It was made in a time where no one could buy the lie anymore—a long, bad war had made that impossible. The album's metaphor of longing, lost innocence and consequence is best illuminated on "Racing in the Streets"—the tale of good people adrift in their betrayal, wanting to "wash the sin off their hands." *Darkness* is the album that established Springsteen as one of the great communicators of the American dilemma; the work of someone born to a country founded on moral covenant, always striving to be that exemplar city on the hill but forever falling shy of its mark.

VEDDERAN: NOTES ON PEARL JAM'S 20TH ANNIVERSARY CONCERT

TINYLUCKYGENIUS, September 2011

So, this weekend, my friend Leor joined me in the car and we drove for two hours to see PEARL JAM in the woods of Wisconsin for 12 hours! It was for work (*Rolling Stone*), but lord knows I love a spectacle and Leor loves Mudhoney, and he was literally the only person I could find with any sort of enthusiasm at the prospect of going to an all-day anniversary festival for old, old Pearl Jam. Pearl Jam, who I never have paid much real attention to, other than I see pictures of Eddie Vedder and think he is not aging a bit and is still rather handsome. Two nights before I watched the Cameron Crowe-directed documentary about the band's 20 years; lord alive, there is not a more earnest and tenderhearted person in rock n' roll than Eddie Vedder, in case you were doubting just how sensitacho he rolls. The part where his bandmates explain that a few records in he seized control of the band and essentially tried to turn the band into Fugazi and that it pretty much almost broke them up was pretty much my favorite part because THERE IS ALWAYS THAT GUY IN EVERY BAND. I was always that guy in all my bands.

Anyhow.

Deep into Wisconsin! We arrived and there were tons of bros and white hats and people keeping the rain out with football team ponchos and slitted trashbags, grilling out of the back of pickups, with serious tents and folding comfortable chairs, and it was like 4 p.m., and there were already people so drunk they'd given up on wearing shoes.

Inside, we went to our seats in the amphitheater. There were not a lot of people braving the rain for Mudhoney. I counted exactly five people who seemed to know the words. I ate a cheeseburger because I had to. Mark Arm, strangely, has not aged. I watched them doing the old hits and some new songs I didn't know (did they put out a record I didn't know about?) and the man was doing his Iggy wiggle and the new stuff all sounded like The Scientists and they closed with a Black Flag cover and I thought "Mark Arm must be doing a lot of yoga." Also, I realized watching them that I think I last saw Mudhoney on the day before my 16th birthday, on the *Every Good Boy* tour, and I was seeing them, still/again on the day before my 35th birthday. I don't know if that is weirder for me or to be them doing that, though being almost 50 and being in Mudhoney is probably a blast.

Around us on the impossible-graded slopes of the amphitheater (it's at a ski resort!) were PJ fans who totally only cared about PJ but soon might be drunk enough to give into something sort of pop-heavy as Queens of the Stone Age, because they were bored (and they did). There were hundreds of people sitting on wet grass in the rain wearing a trash bag that was squishing them so they looked like a blackened SpongeBob and gulping down $13 neon margarita-frosties from concessions that were served in foot-tall guitar shaped cups, limp and slackened by booze, numb in Vedder-ticipation. The amount that dudes in our aisle were coming and going to the beer stands past our seat was like 4–5 times a set, for $14 tallboys. I do not think ever in my life I have been around so many people who were so actively wasted for such a duration, and I have been to SXSW several times.

And then, like three hours into our adventure, The Strokes played. I would think for some reason they would a be a little urban(e) and effete for this Midwestern crowd, but people were into it, even before Vedder guested on "Juicebox."

AND THEN THEN, Dennis Rodman walked into the crowd in-between sets and people freaked out and it was strange. I saw no other celebrity, though I am sure maybe one more was there.

AND FINALLY, The Pearl Jam played. And played no hits, and played for almost three hours, and it was a real roller coaster. Mike McCready is truly one of the blandest guitar players I have ever heard. It is a testament to the rest of the band and especially Eddie Vedder that they 1. have the patience, as seasoned music fans, to sit through his soloing, which is both tepid and colorless, and 2. that they have hits in spite of his totally generic playing. But then again, I guess that is often how things get on the radio, so maybe that's a lesser point. Also, it was smart of Mike McCready to not wear a spaghetti strap tank top like he did at PJ's 10th anniversary. At least they seem to be through their decade-long bad hats phase.

Vedder is so straight in his connection to the audience, he's Spring-steen-ian in that regard, but without the rock 'n' roll showman part. He's understated, the anti-rock-god rock god and that's why people love him. It's impossible not to watch him and eat it up. It feels good to do so. His banter is absolutely corny, like he is 15 and trying to explain *why* he loves playing music. He is letting that part of him do the talking. Which is awesome and also really funny. More people should do that.

AND THEN THEN THEN: Chris Cornell came out, and lord, he has such lovely posture, and they did some Temple of the Dog songs and though I never liked that band, I reconsidered them for those 20 minutes and was impressed. Also, Vedder and Cornell are both freakishly well-preserved, especially when presented together. Everyone else looks like the Cryptkeeper in comparison. I bet there is an Internet underworld of Temple of the Dog slash fiction starring them. I don't even want to Google that.

GRUNGE RETURNED AND I SAW IT.

YOU'RE RELIVING ALL OVER ME: DINOSAUR JR. REUNITES

Chicago Reader, **April 2005**

It was about an hour after dusk in the early summer of 1991, and I was sitting on a log in the half-woods near my parents' house with a guy I'd met in the front row at a Dinosaur Jr. show. I had the names of my favorite bands scrawled in pen on the toe caps of my Converse high-tops ("Fugazi" on the left, "Dinosaur" on the right), and I studied them intently, trying to keep my teenage awkwardness under control. Two dorks alone in the dark, we avoided the obvious question by engaging in deep conversation: *Was Dinosaur Jr. better with or without Lou Barlow?*

I'd hung out with this guy a few times, and every night was the same: as he rattled off Dinosaur Jr. minutiae, I'd nod attentively, hoping that'd charm him. He was one of two boys who would actually talk to me. I was 16, but I still had braces and could easily pass for 12. I also knew more about Dinosaur Jr. (and all his other favorite bands) than he did, but I kept that to myself. If I intimidated him, he wouldn't want to sit on area logs with me anymore. I decided to act docile and tried not to show my teeth when I laughed.

Maybe it was particular to the time and place—Minneapolis in the early '90s—but from what my girlfriends told me, lots of boys thought going to the woods with a girl and regaling her with an hour and a half of Dinosaur Jr. trivia was a perfectly acceptable courtship ritual. If you liked him (or Dinosaur Jr.) enough, you could pretend it was a date. I withstood many hours of Dinologue during those awful teen years, and my memories of the band's early albums—with their noisy, shimmery solos and shots of warm feedback—are inextricably tied to memories of some dude that never liked me back. Actually, there was a series of dudes—they only seem to blend into one because they all shared the same bell-shaped, grunge-bob hairstyle, unflagging devotion to J Mascis, and polite disinterest in me.

Dinosaur Jr.'s first three full-lengths, *Dinosaur* (Homestead, 1985), *You're Living All Over Me* (SST, 1987), and *Bug* (SST, 1988), have only been out of print for five years or so and have never been too hard to find on eBay or used bins. Nonetheless, on March 22, Merge Records reissued all of them. They're the only albums with the band's original lineup: guitarist and frontman Mascis, one-named drummer Murph, and bassist Barlow, who quit (or was fired) in 1989. Barlow subsequently dedicated himself to the tape-hiss horn of plenty Sebadoh, which he'd started as a side project a couple years before, and Mascis and Murph soldiered on with a rotating cast of bassists. In 1990, Dinosaur signed with Sire, and the following year they issued the flawless *Green Mind*.

The band was rumored to have become a Mascis dictatorship—an impression confirmed in the reissues' liner notes—and by the mid-'90s Murph was gone, too. Until Sire dropped Dinosaur in 1997, Mascis and a lineup of scabs rewarded a devoted fan base with diminishing returns. Then Mascis became The Fog, a studio project that only turned into a proper band to tour. He receded into the distance, dwindling to a speck on the horizon—if you'd been able to make him out, you'd still have seen his long hair, his guitar, and his flannel, but he'd lost his spot on the main stage to other dudes, dudes with turntables, who were to become our newest heroes.

In the late '80s, though, Dinosaur were magnets for the devotion of teenage weirdos, combining the huge, thralling Marshall-stack overdrive that made Neil Young famous with the jacked-up amphetamine-pulse of hardcore. Like their SST labelmates Hüsker Dü, they connected punk's mosh-pit machismo to its brooding, emotional side. Often the hiccuping pummel of the rhythm section would pause, as though Murph and Barlow were trying to fake us out, and then Mascis' guitar would rumble to life, wonderfully too loud, every note gloriously destroyed by the city of effects pedals at his feet. Unlike early punk rockers, Dinosaur weren't lashing out at the bloated, coked-up corpse of the '70s. They were just trying, as Mike Watt suggests in the new liner notes to *You're Living All Over Me*, to be an East Coast version of acid-damaged country punks the Meat Puppets. Save for Mascis' drawling whine, there isn't much country in Dinosaur's music, but it's plenty damaged.

Dinosaur structured their tunes like miniature, wank-free, classic-rock epics. "No Bones," the second cut on *Bug*, begins as an instrumental dirge with the bass playing distorted chords against a skipping, waltzy beat, segues into a verse where Mascis sounds like the loneliest, most congested kid in all of Massachusetts, and from there jumps to a chorus overlaid with a track of strummy acoustic guitar. On the strength of songs like this, Mascis became not just a fanboy icon but an icon's icon—Sonic Youth's "Teenage Riot," from the 1988 album *Daydream Nation*, is reputedly about his dominion over the guitar and the kids.

In their lyrics, Dinosaur don't even toy with the nihilistic slogan-eering of many of their progenitors and peers. Mascis' singing is endearingly amateurish, his voice gentle, his diction thick, his lyrics vague. He never adopts an obvious pose or persona, but his words don't reveal much about who he is; maybe he's being honest, but he's not being particularly forthcoming. In short lines capped with simple rhymes, he often sketches a blurry metaphor about what stands between him and her—listening to this stuff is like reading a teenager's frustrated, lovelorn poetry, written for an audience of one. Even when Mascis is singing his most somnambulant monotone, his voice cracks whenever he hits the word "girl." Barlow barely ever takes the mic, but his one star turn on *Bug* is a doozy. On "Don't," he howls with the consuming rage of 10,000 virginal high school seniors: "Why? / Why don't you like me?" Those are the only lyrics, and he repeats them 44 times—it's emo distilled to its essence.

In Dinosaur's songs, the topic is often romance, but it's hard to tell whether the girl said yes or no or if she never got asked a question in the first place. That fumbling dorkiness is a big part of the charm. It's easy to imagine that the band spent puberty the same way a lot of their fans probably did: perched on the edge of their bed playing along with metal records on a shitty Ibanez, growing out their hair, smoking weed, and getting ignored by their crush. Dinosaur have bastardized everything from folky pop to feral thrash to turgid classic rock, imbuing it with qualities sacred to the indie-rock fanboy: a nerd's aesthetic, virtuosity, and emotionally fraught lyrics. Their albums nodded to the most righteous parts of your record collection, and the songs were open-ended enough that they could easily be about you and your ennui. In the late '80s, Dinosaur helped create a template that Nirvana would take worldwide when "Teen Spirit" went nuclear a few years later.

Considering how much indie rock has changed since 1986, do these three Dinosaur reissues belong anywhere now? *Bug* is a great record but feels irrelevant in the harsh light of the current post-post-post-punk world, with its skinny ties and drum machines and leg warmers and hedonism. The twenty-year-old snapshots included in the reissues' beefed-up liner notes reveal three greasy-looking dudes who wouldn't have made it past the door at a loft party in Brooklyn in 2005—they've got teenage trauma in their eyes and look like they've probably never seen a tit in real life.

These three lost-looking dorkboys made totally monstrous records, though: sprawling, adolescent, and sharp. Dinosaur's early albums were casually elaborate and masterfully sloppy. Unfortunately, the timing of the band's long-rumored reunion—for their first gig together since 1989, Mascis, Murph and Barlow are playing the Late Late Show on CBS on April 15 (followed by European and U.S. tours) makes the reissues seem opportunistic. Given the epic bad blood between Mascis and Barlow, their reconciliation seems too convenient to look like anything but a cash-in. Why couldn't they stick to pursuing their increasingly marginal solo careers, leaving us to savor our memories of the great shit they did together back in the day?

At least one beautiful thing might come of this. If Dinosaur's mid-life crisis reunion repels enough of the kids who might've fallen in love with these reissues, it could save a generation of teen punk girls from hours of distortion-pedal discourse on awkward dates in the woods.

YOU WILL ACHE LIKE I ACHE: THE ORAL HISTORY OF HOLE'S *LIVE THROUGH THIS*

SPIN magazine, April 2014

It's hard not to work through the what-if's of *Live Through This*. What if the world had gotten a proper introduction to this album? What if we only had to confront the image of Courtney Love the rock star that week, rather than the Courtney Love we saw in grief, giving away her husband's T-shirts to mourning teens? How would we have understood such an iconic album, if it had not been bracketed by Kurt Cobain's suicide? And what would Hole have become if bassist Kristen Pfaff had lived?

That it made its way outside of the long shadow of death is testament to just how masterful *Live Through This* was and is—an incontrovertible work that Love and her band fought to bring into the word, to legitimize themselves as a band and worthy peers to Nirvana, Smashing Pumpkins, and the sensitive boy-geniuses of the alt-rock era. It is a ferocious album that ultimately broke through on the strength of "Doll Parts," a song so tender it crushes you, a song written years earlier but transmogrified later by collective mourning. Love gave us these wrought anthems, and in them we saw her genius and the absolute power of the band; we reveled in finally having a female icon blessed with the cocksure strut and don't-give-a-fuck of rock's true greats. Love's surety of her band's rightful place in the hierarchy was permission writ large for every girl with a guitar. She was compelling, terrifying and incandescent, and *Live Through This* was the portrait of a woman claiming her power.

But for too long, the story of *Live Through This* and the true impact of the album have been overshadowed by rumors and theories conjured by Kurt-truthers. Here, for your edification and grunge nostalgia, is an accounting of what really happened and how *Live Through This* came into being, according to the people who made it.

Courtney Love, singer/guitarist: Our first record [1991's *Pretty on the Inside*] wasn't supposed to be melodic. It was supposed to be a really raw expression. It wasn't designed to sell any records. It was designed to be cool, really. And I don't mean that in a super-contrived way, but sort of contrived. We had a skeletal band, not very skilled. The next record was going to be more commercial.

Eric Erlandson, guitarist: During the tour for *Pretty on the Inside*, we had been going more pop, less journal-entry noise stuff. The whole industry was going, like, "Look, you can be melodic and punky and be successful!" We never said "Let's do *this*, let's copy *this* formula." It was natural.

Courtney Love: I was very competitive with Kurt [Cobain] because I wanted more melody. But I already wanted that before *Live Through This*.

Eric Erlandson: Courtney brought that pressure about competing with *Nevermind*. I thought that none of that's gonna matter. What matters is just that we make as good of a record as we can with *our* songs.

Mark Kates, A&R at Geffen Records: When Gary Gersh left DGC around May of 1993, I became Hole's A&R person. There was no question that there was skepticism within the company about Hole, to be honest. Anytime you sign an artist that has notoriety, some people are going to look at it differently. As far as looking forward to working on it, it's hard to say. You have to sort of go back in time, and yes, we knew Courtney as Kurt's wife but this wasn't about that. It was never—sadly, unfortunately —about that.

Patty Schemel, drummer: That was *always* the thing looming, that her marriage and her life was bigger than our band. We always had that battle of having to prove ourselves as a legitimate band. All we had were those songs. That was it.

Courtney Love: Kurt got me Patty. I wanted to fire Jill [Emery, Hole's original bassist] but I still liked Caroline [Rue, Hole's first drummer]. Kurt made this whole lecture to me about that fundamental fact in rock 'n' roll that I really didn't know, which is that your drummer is the most important person in your band. Patty fit in perfectly.

Eric Erlandson: Kurt was like, "We're moving to Seattle but we have to have the baby down here [in Los Angeles], so you go up to

Seattle and start working with Patty and we'll meet you there later." I moved to Seattle in May or June of 1992. And of course, they didn't move up until 1993, so I was flying back-and-forth between L.A. and Seattle the whole time.

Patty Schemel: Eric and I were practicing all the time; we set up out in Carnation, Washington at Kurt and Courtney's house out in the woods. We worked while Courtney was pregnant and having Frances and going through that whole drama with *Vanity Fair*. That was a tense time; I was drinking a lot. So there was party time and there was also the time that me and Eric spent re-learning the back catalog.

Courtney Love: The songwriting process was really easy. We started at [defunct L.A. punk club] Jabberjaw. I wrote "Violet" there. Then we moved to Seattle in the middle of that. "Miss World" was written in Seattle, if I remember correctly. Look, I don't even remember who I don't like anymore. My brain is a little addled in terms of my long-term memory. It could be PTSD, which is everyone's excuse for everything. But anyway, Jabberjaw was the salad days of it all. I wrote "Doll Parts" in Cambridge, Massachusetts in a woman named Joyce's bathroom. That one was easy.

Patty Schemel: Me and Courtney came up with "She Walks" in the laundry-room studio in their house and put it together when we went to Rockin' in Rio [with Nirvana]. [Nirvana was recording demos with their sound engineer Craig Montgomery] and when they were done working on ideas for *In Utero*, Courtney and I went in and worked on stuff. We did the idea for "Miss World" and "She Walks." Big John from [U.K. punk band] The Exploited came up with the middle section of "She Walks." He was the guitar tech for Nirvana, and he was like, "Why don't we go at half-time, at that part?" Me and Courtney went up to San Francisco when Kurt was working with the Melvins on *Lysol*. We went in and messed around, and came up with "Jennifer's Body."

Courtney Love: We had this great rehearsal space [in Seattle]: It was just perfect, up on Capitol Hill, near the Urban Outfitters. Everyone got really close. There was just a great flow. This all came about after the whole *Vanity Fair* thing and all the stuff with the baby. Those rehearsals were a really great escape from all that shit;

the only way to escape it was drugs and music.

Eric Erlandson: It was a refuge. It was an emotional time for Courtney and Kurt. I was involved in their drama and was trying to hold it together and replace members and get a record together. So how did I feel emotionally? I was a wreck.

Patty Schemel: Courtney would come in and add vocals and her guitar ideas—which were great—and Eric would fine-tune her ideas and make them amazing. But her initial guitar ideas were really, really cool. That's what Hole is: that sound of Eric's guitar and Courtney's vocals. Hole isn't Hole without those two together.

Eric Erlandson: Even if it was just the three of us playing, you could tell something was happening that was bigger than all of us.

Courtney Love: The rehearsals just flowed. On this record, we didn't really need anyone to help us.

Mark Kates: It's one of my clearest memories ever from doing A&R, going up to see them rehearse in Seattle, and I thought, "There's an album here." I think it was always going to be great—it was just a question of how great.

Courtney Love: I put a lot of energy into the music because it was the place I could put my energy. And the title of the record is not a prediction of the future. It's, like, fucking live through what I already lived through, you motherfuckers! It wasn't meant to be about anybody dying. It was about going through fucking media humiliations like this. You try it—because it ain't fun.

Patty Schemel: Being a wife and being a mother, and all the drama that came with that; being a feminist, and then being known as Mrs. Kurt? I think a lot of all of that frustration and competitiveness went into lyrics, went into the force behind that record.

Eric Erlandson: I found Kristen [Pfaff, bassist] in L.A. and said, "Come with me to meet Courtney and Patty when you get to Seattle." She joined the band, she moved to Seattle, and that's when all the songs came to life, literally. She was the star of her band and so she was bringing that to Hole and that created sparks in everybody;

we all saw an even greater potential than before.

Mark Kates: I remember sitting in that very small rehearsal room, watching them and thinking, "No one knows how great this is. No one I work with has any idea how great an album this is going to be." That was really special. I knew it would blow people away.

Patty Schemel: She was in a band called Janitor Joe. We saw her play, and she was *amazing*. She was just cool. Her playing was heavy, and she was knowledgeable, and she had command of her instrument. When she played, that was it: We knew.

Sean Slade, engineer and producer: When we got the *Live Through This* demos, I realized very quickly that Hole had gotten a new rhythm section—it was much more musical.

Courtney Love: Kristen was just really, really, really good. She had studied music, studied cello. She couldn't do backup vocals. And that was okay because her playing was like, *you know*.

Eric Erlandson: I kept on making her listen to the Beatles to expand out of that driving, aggressive boy-rock that was big in Minnesota at the time. Kristen was very into that. We got into fights over it. And I'd be like, "I like that, too, but you've gotta pretend you're Paul McCartney playing a country song right now."

Patty Schemel: There was such a confidence in her playing that it just all happened, as soon as she started to play. It was really natural for her. "Plump" was one of her ideas.

Courtney Love: I was really anti-heroin while we were working. And everyone did heroin anyway. If you recall.

Patty Schemel: Kristen became Eric's girlfriend, so they were tight. They had each other. Then there was me and my addiction with alcohol and drugs. Kristen and I would get together, and we were always trying to keep the amount of drugs we were doing secret. "Don't tell Eric." There were so many secrets. We were all frustrated, and we all had a lot of downtime. And so to deal with that, there was a lot of "hanging out." I was frustrated. I wanted to play. I wanted to record.

Eric Erlandson: Kristen came on tour with us in Europe [in 1993] and we did a few festivals and a few shows, and there's people going nuts for a song that's not even on record yet.

Patty Schemel: At the Phoenix Festival, we were playing all these brand new songs and there was just this sea of people moving up and down. It was amazing. Kristen was so great live. That was the one tour that we had Kristen on, but it was a glimpse of what was to come.

Mark Kates: I went to England with them in July of '93, and saw them at the Phoenix Festival and I remember walking backstage after this show and saying, "It really doesn't matter who's gonna produce your record because it's gonna be great."

Courtney Love: I wanted to be better than Kurt. I was really competing with Kurt. And that's why it always offends me when people would say, "Oh, he wrote *Live Through This*." I'd be proud as hell to say that he wrote something on it, but I wouldn't let him. It was too Yoko for me. It's like, "No fucking way, man! I've got a good band, I don't fucking need your help."

Eric Erlandson: I knew there was that competitiveness inside Courtney. Because he's so talented, but at the same time, *not* wanting him involved. She had that conflict inside her. I had the same problem, I had the same desire. Wanting to work with him and also not wanting him to touch our art. It's so different than Nirvana: our energy, Courtney and my—our thing that we had been building. It's so different from Nirvana. I didn't want that inside; I didn't want the wrong influences to come in.

Courtney Love: I'm listening to the Breeders' *Pod* 24/7 and I'm listening to the Pixies 24/7 and I'm listening to Echo & the Bunnymen and Joy Division. I come from a different place [than Kurt]. It wasn't like I was just taking from Billy [Corgan, Smashing Pumpkins frontman] and Kurt. I was taking from my own influences, hugely.

Eric Erlandson: We never finished writing; we were writing the whole time, trying to come up with more and more songs because even though it looked like we had a good, solid album, we knew we were missing some pieces. We were still writing intensely and frantically putting songs together. It wasn't like, "Oh we have these 12 songs, they're done, and we're going to go in and record now." It's never been like that with this band.

Sean Slade: There were only a handful of songs on the *Live Through This* demo—four, five at max. We liked to hear as many songs as we can before we say yes or no to an album. But, in this case, the four or the five songs we heard sounded good enough.

Paul Q. Kolderie, producer and engineer: Early on in the process, we got a demo from Mark Kates and it completely blew my mind. A lot of times in my career, you hear something and you just know. When I heard the lyrics to "Doll Parts," I just thought, "This is going to be big."

Courtney Love: I don't know why we picked Paul and Sean. Because [Hole manager] Janet Billig told me to? Because they'd produced The Lemonheads? I didn't really think much about producers at the time.

Eric Erlandson: We picked Paul and Sean because Kurt would just sit there and watch MTV all day, and he's like, "Get the guy that did the Green Day album." [*Laughs.*] Those were the videos that were on all the time then. It was Radiohead's "Creep," and then Green Day. I remember him saying, "Get the Green Day producer or get the Radiohead guy." I don't know what happened with the Green Day guy, but for some reason we got Sean and Paul.

Patty Schemel: I don't know why we picked them; I guess maybe because of that Radiohead record, I'm not sure.

Mark Kates: Courtney was kind of obsessed with getting either Brendan O'Brien [producer of Pearl Jam's *Vs.*] or Butch Vig to produce the album and neither was really responding. People who had done multi-platinum records.

Courtney Love: I didn't go to [Smart Studios, in Madison, Wisconsin] with Butch. I didn't want to go down that road and copy Kurt.

Paul Q. Kolderie: I was at [Boston-area recording studio] Fort Apache and I got a call from Butch Vig's manager, Shannon O'Shea, and she said, "You don't know me, but I did you a favor." I asked, "You wanna tell me any more about what it is?" And she says, "No, let's leave it at that and see what happens." Courtney and Kurt were meeting with Butch to see if he wanted to do it, since Butch did *Nevermind*, but Butch was tired after doing *Siamese Dream* and he wanted to work on what turned out later to be Garbage. He wasn't up for a Courtney record. Shannon said, "Why don't you get the guys that did 'Creep?'" And Mark Kates said, "I can get you those guys."

Sean Slade: Courtney was aware of us probably because of the Dinosaur Jr. connection, because Kurt was not only a fan of Dinosaur Jr., but at one point J Mascis was considering playing drums in Nirvana. I remember her referring to us as the "Boston guys."

Paul Q. Kolderie: We had a phone conversation with Courtney that went pretty well. She didn't really ask us about anything, we just talked about the Lyres and bands from Boston that she was obsessed with. I remember, embarrassingly, she was talking about *Let It Be* and how she loved that record, and I said, "Oh, yeah, the Beatles are cool." And she was like, "No, I'm talking about the Replacements." I thought I had lost the gig right there.

Mark Kates: I remember it vividly. It was my idea. One day we were on a conference call: me, Courtney and Janet Billig. Those guys were old friends of mine. I mentioned them tentatively, I didn't know if anyone knew who they were, but I knew that the first Radiohead record was popular in Kurt and Courtney's house. And I mentioned Sean and Paul, and Courtney goes, "Wow, Boston. The Lyres." I mean, it wasn't even a band they had worked with, but she was very aware of the lineage of the music she was part of. The next thing we did was put them on the phone. And then it happened.

Courtney Love: Went to [Triclops Sound Studios, in Marietta, Georgia] because Billy made *Siamese Dream* there. And I loved the way that it sounds.

Paul Q. Kolderie: I went out to Seattle and did pre-production with just the band; Courtney wasn't around. They had already hired us at that point. Courtney told us that she felt like she was getting two guys for the same price and she liked that. We picked the studio because Butch had been there with the Pumpkins and Courtney was convinced that we had to have a Neve board and Studer tape recorders, which were top of the line. We were thinking about Muscle Shoals, but she called Billy or Butch and talked to them about it and that's how we wound up in Atlanta.

Eric Erlandson: Kurt had just made *In Utero*, he got all these notes about mics and guitars and the studio set-up and everything. He mapped out this whole diagram and it said, "This is what you should do in the studio." Of course, that all went out the window. The one thing that made it was this all-metal guitar that I borrowed from some guitar shop in Washington—Kurt suggested that one guitar.

Courtney Love: [Cobain biographer] Charlie Cross found this document—it's credited as Kurt's drum map, except it's not Kurt's handwriting, it's mine. It's Kurt's studio drum map, the mics to use and Billy's [studio drum map]; I combined the two of them.

Sean Slade: About when we started getting the drum sounds Courtney called Butch Vig. She had been hanging out at Pachyderm, where Nirvana had just finished *In Utero* with Albini. And Albini is very opinionated about drum sounds. [*Laughs.*] I guess Courtney really wanted Butch for *Live Through This*, but he was unavailable, and the only time she ever really got involved with what we were doing was when she came in when we were setting up drums and said, "What mics are you using?" I explained that we were using this on this drum, this mic on this drum. "Well, what's on the snare?" "We're using a Shure 57." And she says, "Albini says Shure 57's suck." I had heard that, but everyone uses a goddamn Shure 57 on the snare drum, okay? But Albini had to say it was for hacks, as if it was an insult to art. And so I said to her, "No, that's not a regular 57, that's a Turbo 57." I made it up. So, she calls Butch and tells him the mics we're using "and a Turbo 57 on the snare." And [I] wasn't privy to his side of it, but he told her those were all great, that we knew what we were doing. There was never any technical issues beyond that. We thanked Butch later for covering for us.

Eric Erlandson: It was the first time Hole had worked with real producers. I was really happy to have somebody outside the band helping [*laughs*] because I was having my ideas shot down.

Sean Slade: We never really talked about any kind of grand artistic vision of *Live Through This* with Courtney. The only memory I have of any kind of goal she had was when she walked into the control room almost crying and said, "This album *has* to go gold."

Sean Slade: That Hole hadn't become stars yet was much to the advantage of the project. They were very focused and very ambitious. The whole world was trying to figure out what Courtney and Hole were gonna come out with on their first major label album. They knew that this had to be a maximum effort.

Eric Erlandson: I was there the most out of everybody. After we recorded the basic track, I set up this wall of amps and would just go in and plug in different ones to different guitars. I remember feeling like a kid in a candy shop.

Patty Schemel: I got my own drum tech, Carl Plaster, who came out and tuned all my drums, perfectly, to notes on the scale, which was *huge* for me. Just different snare drum options was a big deal; just having the resources to have different drum sounds was cool. I remember getting "Jennifer's Body" on the second take because I loved playing that song so much.

Sean Slade: Kristen was just amazing. She's such a natural talent, knew exactly what to play, played totally tight with Patty. I have to give her credit—and this has never happened on an album that we've done in all these years—every single bass track on *Live Through This* was from the basic tracks. There was no bass overdubs because there was no need to because they were perfect. It was an exceptional performance on her part. That's like a singer doing an album's worth of vocals in just one take. It just doesn't happen.

Paul Q. Kolderie: Kristen is the secret ingredient; she made the whole thing gel and happen. It's criminal she didn't get to make any more records because it would have been great to see what came down the road.

Courtney Love: Half the fucking songs were written in the studio.

Sean Slade: We witnessed "Asking for It" from when it didn't exist to when it got finished. It was fascinating. There was a certain magic going on.

Paul Q. Kolderie: I always bring that up whenever people say "Kurt wrote the songs"—I can say he didn't because *I watched it happen.*

Sean Slade: At one point Courtney was working out lyrics and she came up with a line that I thought wasn't that good and I said, "Ah, that's not happening," and she goes, "Sean, you're not my English teacher." And I looked at her and said, "But, Courtney, I *am*," and she laughed. It's rare to ever get someone with that level of lyrical talent. I stand in awe of that. When you are able to work with someone who is on that level, that literary level, who stands as a writer—it's an honor.

Courtney Love: We collaborated really well. I just think we had really good chemistry, to be honest.

Paul Q. Kolderie: You know those cartoon things where when people are fighting and there is a dust cloud with sparks and stars flying out? That's how I think of it. There was always a fight about something. There were ashtrays flying. But they were never fighting with us. We would shut the control room door. We'd send them home and just work.

Eric Erlandson: There was a lot of tension going on. There's tension in the room whenever we got together. *And* there's tension between Kristen and I because we had been living together and seeing each other and then she moved out. We were having this difficult, on-and-off relationship, and we go to Atlanta to record and we have to room together.

Sean Slade: Kristen and Eric had just broken up, so there was interpersonal weirdness there. But when they were in the studio they were focused on getting the work done. Despite all of Courtney's idiosyncrasies, she's really, really smart and she was there to work hard.

Patty Schemel: During basic tracks, me and Courtney ended up leaving and going to New York to see Nirvana on Saturday Night Live. I was so drunk that I could not see straight. It was so fucked up. RuPaul was there. And I remember coming back and then having to do more recording and being completely wasted for that. When I got back, I was like, "I gotta pull it together." So that's when I did a bunch of crystal meth. We pretty much finished up our basic tracks and then we were kind of imbibing.

Paul Q. Kolderie: The studio was in the middle of an office park in suburban Atlanta. The only place you could get anything to eat was a Fuddruckers or TGI Fridays. There was nothing else to do but work on the record.

Mark Kates: I remember Courtney staying at the Hotel Nikko, and I was driving her to the studio one day and we passed a billboard for Hooters, which I think was still a regional chain, and she goes, "Hooters? Is that like a strip club for the whole family?"

Courtney Love: We recorded all the time. We'd go to this one club called Heaven and Hell and I think we debuted some of the songs there, and people were screaming, "Shut up!" It's like, "Fuck you, you little fucking punk rats." But I came to this conclusion a long time ago: "Selling out" means there are no more tickets at Madison Square Garden.

Sean Slade: The label put us up in a crappy corporate condo with rented furniture and no art on the walls next door to a coke dealer; it was almost deserted.

Mark Kates: The studio was in a strip mall next to an insurance place.

Courtney Love: Me and Patty shared a room and Kristen and Eric shared a room in this apartment complex. We went to work every day and had something to look forward to. We were making good music in a good studio. It was fun.

Sean Slade: We got the basic tracks in about four or five days, so from that point on our schedule revolved around accommodating Courtney's approach to the studio. We quickly discovered that if you ask her to be at any place at any given time she would always be two hours late. But two hours late *to the minute*. And she couldn't be fooled, either. Knowing she was going to be two hours late, if you wanted her to be there at 4, if you told her to be there at 2, she would show up at 6.

Paul Q. Kolderie: Nirvana was on tour and Kurt would call and ask us to hold the phone up so he could hear what was going on. There were a lot of crazy distractions. We kept our heads down and kept working.

Patty Schemel: Courtney ended up moving into a five-star hotel for the rest of the time we were there. I was like, "Uh, I'm cool where I'm at." But she's like, "Well, come over and have room service." One morning, I was with her and she got a phone call and was like, "Oh my god: River Phoenix died last night." So, that was a full day of her talking to people on the phone.

Sean Slade: They rarely brought the weirdness into the control room. And occasionally I would wander out and hang out with them, I would experience it, but it never really bugged me—what we were coming up with had such emotional force.

Eric Erlandson: Sean and Paul were good at pep-talking me like, "You don't realize that if you just relaxed, and just accepted that you're good and not be insecure about it, then you'd be better." I felt like everything I was playing was pretty much horrible. I had never played acoustic guitar, but I knew I had to use it on "Doll Parts." So I'm playing this 12-string acoustic and I can't even press down on my strings. "What is this? What am I supposed to do with it?"

Sean Slade: Eric was like Eeyore. I told him it wasn't very rock 'n' roll—the spirit of it is really about reckless confidence and going with your gut instinct, not about wringing your hands.

Paul Q. Kolderie: It wasn't an easy band to be in if you weren't Courtney; she expected a lot from them. She sometimes expected them to know what she wanted even when she had not been real clear about it. She wouldn't say what to do; more what not to do. Eric took it personally.

Sean Slade: We set up every evening for Courtney to do vocals and she would sing two or three songs, multiple takes of each song. And she put in a lot of intensity and emotion. Then, at a certain point, maybe about 10 or 11, she was done. So, the next day Paul and I would come in each morning and spend three or four hours editing and putting them together. We did that every day for about two and a half weeks until we had tracked the album that way, very methodically.

Paul Q. Kolderie: She didn't talk about competing with Kurt. The Pumpkins were at their peak and Nirvana was the biggest band in the world, but she was feeling like she was as good as either of those guys.

Courtney Love: I think it's pretty flawless for what it is, for the time. For going from *Pretty on the Inside*, which is atonal and has really brilliant lyrics, to fucking songs you can sing along to? I just gave it my best. I gave it 100 percent.

Sean Slade: Paul and I had different ideas about what was going on. He was very depressed; he thought the album was coming out awful. Whereas I thought that it was coming out great. I came to terms with, or accepted, Courtney's idiosyncrasies a lot better than he did. I thought her craziness was somewhat of a put-on, a defense mechanism to keep the world at bay.

Paul Q. Kolderie: Kurt showed up during a break from tour, got in late and then came to the studio the next morning. We chatted for a bit, he wanted to hear the record and we played him all the tracks. He was complimentary; he liked the drum sounds, thought the songs were great. Then Courtney said, "Let's go in," and they're both sitting in front of the vocal mic, and she said, "I want you to sing some harmonies." And he said, "I can't sing harmonies until I hear the songs; I don't even know the songs." We played the song through a few times; he may have been loaded, but I had just met him so I don't know what he was like. He put a few things on. If you listen carefully, maybe you can hear it.

Courtney Love: Kurt came to Triclops and he sang on one song, and I mixed it up and released it, so you can hear him sing on one song. But that's it.

Eric Erlandson: Kurt showed up; he's not in any good condition at that point. He was not in a good place.

Patty Schemel: I remember he was on so much Klonopin, too, and it was like "*What* is going on?" I remember he did some stuff on

"Asking for It." They were just messing around.

Eric Erlandson: He didn't know any of the songs, there were drugs involved, and Courtney's like, "Change something on this." Mainly just to get some harmonies, I guess. Not anything about the writing of the songs, not anything with even the vocal melodies. Everything was already done. He was going in there mumbling harmonies over a couple songs. Those things were not used on the album; they turned up in a mix later. You can hear him on top of whatever song that was—I think "Softer, Softest"—but he was never actually *involved*.

Sean Slade: I had one conversation with Kurt when we were mixing it. Courtney called and said, "Kurt wants to talk to you." And I remember looking at Paul and Paul giving me a look like, "You're gonna do this one." I got on the phone and Kurt starts going, "I got these mixes, and here's what you gotta do—you gotta make the snare sound huge, and you gotta double all of Courtney's vocals." And I said, "Sorry, Kurt, but we're not gonna do that. That's not the album we are making here, that's not the approach we're taking." What Kurt was saying, basically, was make it sound like my album, make it sound like *Nevermind*. And I told him, straight up, no way, we're not going to do that. I probably pissed him off, but I didn't care.

Paul Q. Kolderie: By the end, communication was at an incredible low point: 42 days straight, working everyday, the pressure cooker. We had the world's biggest rock star coming in and saying he didn't like this sound or he did. We wanted to just mix and get out of there. We felt like the writing was on the wall—we thought Kurt was going to take it and mix it with Scott Litt. It's what they'd done with *In Utero*. I didn't care who mixed it; I was just done.

Patty Schemel: I enjoyed playing all of those songs, and I felt comfortable, and I felt at ease, and I felt excited about all of the songs. I think I remember Sean or Paul saying, "Oh, this will be a great punk record"—you know, not giving it its full due. It was weird because I was so proud of the record, but it was hard to get any perspective being so close to Nirvana. Everything they did was huge, so it was hard to get any idea of what our record would do. I was so proud of it. And that was all that mattered to me at that time.

Courtney Love: I didn't feel like I nailed that, but I nailed my own version of it. I feel fine about it. I have a pretty healthy self-esteem. Sometimes. I didn't think it was as good as *Siamese Dream*, I didn't think it was as good as *Nevermind*, but I thought it was fucking damn good.

Paul Q. Kolderie: We were up so close to it, we couldn't see what a great album it was. She wanted to make a record as good as *Siamese Dream* or *Nevermind*, and we were trying our hardest, but we didn't know how to do that. There is no secret formula. Sometimes it happens, and sometimes it doesn't. In this case, it did.

Eric Erlandson: One thing: Wikipedia is so wrong. I just read the whole *Live Through This* Wikipedia thing, and it's so wrong.

Patty Schemel: Oh, so full of shit, that Wikipedia. France? We didn't go to France. That's a load of shit.

Courtney Love: I had a plan for the fourth record, and the fifth record, and the sixth record. I had a really grand design that got messed with because of my own problems. But I made it all the way to the third record, which absolutely, exactly was my vision. I'm not quite sure why *Live Through This* is so iconic. I think it's because girls don't make angry records as much. I've always thought [PJ Harvey's] *Rid of Me* was a far superior record than *Live Through This*, but that's good—it just keeps my ego in check.

YOU KNOW WHAT?
TINYLUCKYGENIUS, April 2010

Older-generation female rocker ladies making uninformed judgment calls about women making music today, and how no one is angry anymore, how the '90s were so much better, when we had Liz Phair and Hole and Belly and L7 on MTV (a.k.a. the blinded nostalgia trope of the aging rock 'n' roll feminist) IS REALLY FUCKING UNPRODUCTIVE.

It also shows they are not digging deep enough, or seeing the forest for the trees. If you think "angry women in punk" is a faction that has somehow receded, or that L7 in its day was some how better than the generation of women now in all manner of metal bands, you've gotten too far removed from the action. Go browse the 7" new arrivals like you did last in 199X and you'll see a lot more women in the bin now than you ever did then. Spend 11.4 minutes online and catch up. It never disappeared, we just missed it because we were so busy clinging tight to copies of *Guyville*; we refused new ideas as relevant or good enough.

Riot-grrrl wasn't the end result, it was the catalyst. That's what it was supposed to be, that's what it was meant as—not a static thing. It didn't have to stick around forever to count as successful—movements come in waves—it did its job perfectly. So much is different post-RG, so much permission and power and inspiration was funneled down steadily—whether it's to the league of young girl shredders, or rock camps, or queer show collectives whose tether to RG was simply catching the tail end of Sleater-Kinney.

Feminism has to move on, salute new icons, be excited by the varieties of archetypes of women in music that are self-directed, self-produced, not operating under the shadow of a Svengali hand. To not appreciate the difference in agency, or appreciate the different struggles of women now, turns it to a game of radical one-upsmanship. Our battles are not to be hung on the necks of the new waves of girls like an albatross.

I remember in about 1995 or '96, reading an interview with Exene Cervenka from X that was really dismissive of "kids today" and the last time I saw her she was on the mini stage at a Girls Rock Camp benefit gushing about how great this was because it was time for a new feminism, and it was great that these young women (and little girls) have it totally different than we did. She can appreciate that because she is paying attention, she is part of it, in staying present in music and accepting new generations on their own terms. She is showing new girls that they are part of a continuum, not just passing on this epic mantle of *the struggle*. The impact of earlier punk feminism is so totally evident in so much music that is happening now, and it needn't replicate what came before or paved the way for it. The sense of permission endowed in the work of women making music today is as radical—if not more so—than if they were parroting Bikini Kill lines. How current feminist work honors older feminist work is with its progress and new paths. That is all we should ask of it as feminists: BLAZE THE FUCK PAST US.

The hope was then, in this supposed '90s golden era that is often harkened back to, that we would move beyond. Not park and roll around in it for another 18 years. The hope was that punk rock world would get better so that we wouldn't always *need* Riot-grrrl to intercede and open everyone's eyes. If we are now fondly recalling Alanis Fucking Morrissette as some sort of speaking-truth-to-power icon over supporting women who are making music today, then punk feminism is in much deeper shit than we ever were.

PART
FOUR

CALIFORNIA

KENDRICK LAMAR: NOT YOUR AVERAGE, EVERYDAY RAP SAVIOR

SPIN magazine, **October 2012**

The story of Kendrick Lamar is not the story of a rapper from Compton. It might be the story of the most important rapper since Jay-Z. It might be the story of how hip-hop got real in 2012. But the only story Kendrick Lamar wants to tell is how he got out. Lamar's major-label debut, *Good Kid, m.A.A.d City*, is a totemic memoir that marks the distance from where he came. It is, says Lamar, about how "everything in the dark comes to light."

On the cover of the album is a Polaroid dating from 1991. Lamar identifies himself as "baby Kendrick," even though he was pushing 5 when it was taken. He sits nestled in the lap of an uncle who is throwing a gang sign with the same arm that's wrapped around his nephew. On the table sits a 40-ounce and a baby bottle; baby Kendrick is wide-eyed, staring directly into the camera. "We got photo books full of pictures like that," he says. "I was in that atmosphere every day until my teenage years."

He picked the photo "for the innocence in that kid's eyes; not knowing that a baby bottle and a 40-ouncer..." He trails off. "It's still so vivid to me. This picture shows how far I really come."

The 25-year-old MC is curled up in a corner of the couch at the back of his tour bus, wearing the pajamas he slept in, hoodie drawn and sleeves yanked over his hands. With the air conditioning on full-blast, the bus feels like a meat locker. Hundreds of fans queue up outside the venue, hours before doors open. It is Lamar's first headlining tour and tonight's show in Chicago is sold out.

Lamar may be from Compton, but his roots are here. Tonight's *entire* 200-person guest list is made up of family, including Lamar's grandpa, one of many relatives he helps support. "I ain't even made my first big purchase yet," he says. "I live in Los Angeles and I don't even have a car. My ends go to take care of my family." He used his Aftermath signing bonus to move his parents out of the Compton neighborhood where they raised him.

Lamar's parents met while they were kids working on Chicago's South Side; his mom was one of 13 kids, his dad one of seven. In 1984, while still teenagers, they moved to Compton in order to start a family away from the gang warfare that was tearing up the city, where Kendrick's dad was affiliated with the Gangster Disciples. "Compton was just as rough, but they didn't know that," explains Lamar. His parents had him three years later, and his three siblings came seven years after that. Lamar's mother also moved much of her family out to Compton as well, effectively transferring their Chicago life to California proper. In Kendrick's earliest memories, his parents are 25, the same age he is now. He shakes his head in disbelief.

"I always play back these house parties in my memory," he says. "Takin' off my shirt and wilin' out with my cousins, getting in trouble for riding our Big Wheels inside the house. They'd be playin' oldies and gangsta rap. Just drinkin' and smokin' and laughter. A young crowd enjoying themselves. They were living the lifestyle."

Growing up, his mom worked in fast food, and his dad did, too, sometimes. "My pops did whatever he could to get money. He was in the streets. You know the story." There were stints of being on welfare. "I remember always walking to the government building with Mom. We got our food stamps fast because we lived across the street," laughs Lamar. "I didn't know it was hard times because they always had my Christmas present under the tree and for my birthday."

It wasn't until middle school when he realized that there was a different kind of normal for kids who weren't growing up in Compton. There were kids from the Valley, north of Hollywood, who were bussed 30 miles to Compton to attend Kendrick's school. "I went over to some of their houses...and it was a whole 'nother world. Family pictures of them in suits and church clothes up everywhere. Family-oriented. Eatin' together at the table. We ate around the TV. Stuff like that; I didn't know nothin' about. Eatin' without your elbows on the table? I'm lookin' around like, 'What is goin' on?!' I came home and asked my mama, 'Why we don't eat 'round the table?' Then I just keep goin', always askin' questions. I think that's when I started to see the lifestyle around us." He pauses and continues. "You always think that everybody live like you do, because you locked in the neighborhood, you don't see no way else."

Lamar says that *Good Kid* is for the kids in those neighborhoods. It's a self-portrait in which others might see themselves. Both of his parents had gang culture in their families, and it was a fundamental part of Lamar's childhood as well. "Being around it, it just seemed like what you gonna do, what you gonna be," he says.

As a teenager he started drinking and partying, emulating and embracing all the things he'd grown up around, until his father sat him down at age 16 and told him something that would alter the course of his young life. "My father said, 'I don't want you to be like me.' I said, '*What you mean you don't want me to be like you?*' I couldn't really grasp the concept." An only child until he was 7, Lamar was, and is, incredibly close to both his parents. His dad took him to the swap meet every weekend for as long as he could remember (a detail that reappears in the song "Westside, Right on Time"), and to see Dr. Dre and Tupac shoot the "California Love" video around the corner from their house; which set off his dreams of being a rapper. "He said, 'Things I have done, mistakes I've made, I never want you to make those mistakes. You can wind up out on the corner.' He knew by the company I keep what I was gettin' into. Out of respect, I really just gathered myself together."

Lamar began to see life around him with new clarity. "I saw the same things over and over. A lot of my homeboys goin' to jail. Not, like, in and out. *Sentences.* And dyin'; it was a constant. It was a gift from God to be able to recognize that."

When you begin to type "Kendrick Lamar" into Google, one of the auto-fill suggestions of popular searches is "Kendrick Lamar gang affiliation," perhaps owing to the assumption that an unaffiliated rapper from the birthplace of gangsta rap seems impossible. Or maybe it speaks to today's skeptical hip-hop fans, who have grown savvy to the frequent disconnect between MCs' images and their real backstory. On the contrary, though, Lamar has several songs refuting that he's ever banged (most notably, "Average Joe," off *Overly Dedicated.*)

He says he's not offended that people may not believe him. "Here's the thing about gangbanging. I was born in that area. Where you have to be affiliated. The difference was I didn't turn 17 and say, 'I wanna be a gang member.' Gangs is my family, I grew up with them, I hung with them. So, I been around it, been through it, but I can't sit here and claim a gang. That's my family more than anything." He smirks, then grows animated, "People saying I am 'gang-affiliated.' Yeah, I almost wanna say that I am because I wanna change the idea. I don't wanna separate myself. I don't wanna be in the hills. I wanna be in the center. I want them to know they can still touch me."

"He's always been humble like that," says Ab-Soul, who has been tight with Lamar since they met eight years ago, and is a member, with Lamar, of the Black Hippy collective. "He hasn't changed. He has a glow about him. He carries it with him; he's just a deep guy." Ab-Soul recalls being humbled by the first time he heard a mixtape recorded under the name "K.Dot." "I was *certain* I was the best MC in my area," he says, laughing. "Or at least my age bracket. But to hear someone rapping at that level at our age, it was incredible."

Lamar began writing rhymes at 13, but it wasn't until he saw 50 Cent's early mixtape success that he realized he could be recording and releasing his rhymes on his own. His first mixtape made its way to Top Dawg Entertainment; the story of his audition has since come to signify his dedication. The 16-year-old MC stepped into the booth and freestyled for two straight hours, while label founder Anthony "Top" Tiffith pretended to ignore him, to see what Lamar had to prove. The label had signed Jay Rock two weeks prior and the two MCs began recording at the label's studio house in nearby Carson. Lamar, then barely 17, was a constant presence after school. In 2009, as the Top Dawg roster had expanded to include Ab-Soul and Schoolboy Q, the foursome formed Black Hippy, "the conglomeration so cool it could freeze L.A." rhymes Lamar on the groups quintessential "Zip That Chop That."

Jay Rock, who is also in Black Hippy, was similarly stunned the first time he went into the studio with Lamar, shortly after they'd both been signed. "I was working on lyrics, writing, writing, writing on paper. And Kendrick goes in the booth with nothing. I asked him where's his paper? He'd written it all—the whole song—in his head in about five minutes. That's when I knew he was crazy. And a genius." Jay Rock cribs the trademark line about Dick Clark to describe Kendrick's maturity level at 17 years old: "He was like the world's oldest teenager."

The first time Ab-Soul was in the studio with Lamar, he saw that he was working on a totally different level. "[Kendrick] was recording full songs with hooks and bridges and melodies and things to keep a crowd. He was not just interested in being the best rapper, he was making songs that the world could sing."

Here's one of the many places where Lamar diverges from the archetype of the "conscious" rapper. He's not enough of any one thing to be categorizable. Sure, he's self-aware and shouts out Marcus Garvey, working in tropes of black liberation without being political. He's got nuanced songs about women with real-life struggles and names, yet plenty of pop-that-pussy cliché. He's emblematic of the purely-for-the-love-of-the-game underground but is also working on a collaboration with Lady Gaga. He broaches all the street shit with a raw emotionalism that signals he's been touched by it. (In a recent interview, he was quoted as saying that the scariest thing he's ever witnessed was someone being shot in the head.) He reanimates narratives about life below the poverty line that we've become desensitized to. His appeal is broad but still nuanced.

Lamar isn't interested in touting himself as moral authority, instead using the story within *Good Kid* as an object lesson that there is another path. Unlike many of hip-hop's previous survivor's-tale albums, *Good Kid* recounts the good old-bad old days—a Reagan-baby born amid poverty, gang war and the crack epidemic—without a trace of nostalgia. He doesn't brandish what he's been through in order to establish how hard he is or to earn street credentials.

And he doesn't think other depictions of the streets are less valid. His family hails from Chicago's 76th Street & Stoney Island, two miles from the O-Block projects where tendentious teen-rap flashpoint Chief Keef grew up. The two are now Interscope labelmates, and the subjects of two of the most sizable bidding wars in recent memory. Keef reportedly pulled down three million, Lamar confirms his deal at 1.7 million. Lamar, who has never met Keef in person, grows emphatic when discussion turns to the moralizing about Keef's songs.

"You can't change where you from," he says. "You can't take a person out of their zone and expect them to be somebody else now that they in the record industry. It's gonna take years. Years of traveling. Years of meeting people. Years of seeing the world." It becomes unclear whether in talking about Keef, Lamar is actually talking about himself. He values Keef's success on the same terms as his own. By doing music, they represent two dudes who are *not* on the streets. "Maybe he'll inspire the next generation to want to do music. Convert that energy to a positive instead of a pistol."

With *Good Kid*, Lamar is also trying to shift how South Central Los Angeles has been portrayed historically on record. "He's telling his truth—the typical story of a kid growing up in Compton," explains Top Dawg's president Terrence "Punch" Henderson. Like everyone around Lamar, Henderson is respectfully mum on what is and isn't on *Good Kid*, but he is clear about how it's a departure. "It's not what you know from N.W.A. It's not about gangs he's representing. It's a classic. The only thing separating him from the greats is time."

That potential is what drew the attention of hip-hop legend Dr. Dre, who signed Lamar to Aftermath after being turned on to a K.Dot mixtape by Eminem's manager (Lamar's Interscope deal also included a label deal for Top Dawg). Dre is one of *Good Kid*'s executive producers and is featured heavily on the album's Twin Sister-sampling lead single "The Recipe" (Lamar also has worked on several tracks for Dre's eternally delayed *Detox*). Lamar smiles broadly when talking about Dre, a fellow graduate of Compton's Centennial High School, who he alternately refers to as his "big homey."

While much has been said (including by Lamar himself) about picking up where his hero Tupac Shakur left off, Dre's patronage cements the extension of that classic '90s West Coast legacy. It's worth noting that the last time Dre ushered a young rapper into the mainstream with such support it was Eminem. So, is the world ready for this next evolution? Kendrick Lamar, the emotionally sober non-gangster? One that doesn't luxuriate in copious consumption or lobster bisque for breakfast? Can you go to the top of the *Billboard* chart with nary a rooster in a 'rari? What if there is no 'rari at all?

Ab-Soul believes that what's on *Good Kid* is universal: "It's Kendrick's story, but it's my story; it's not just an L.A. album. Everyone will get an understanding of why my generation is acting the way they are: violence, vulgarity, anguish, and resentment, rebelliousness, and eff the police. He puts it all in perspective. Not just 'black-on-black crime,' telling the whole story of homies we all had."

While *Good Kid* is pure autobiography, like much of Lamar's work, it's allegorical. While he is rapping about himself, his songs are heavy on experiences and feelings that are universal and easily relatable. It's hard to imagine him ever dropping a song about his jewelry or creeping towards itemized receipt rap. The closest archetype is, perhaps, Jay-Z: the swaggering good guy, the kid that got out. Lamar is separate, peerless in his ability (he never rides the beat the same way twice) and also in the space that he occupies; he's different from previous rap saviors—he's not a scold and his hooks are tantamount to the message. Though, more than all of this is, what defines Lamar is that he's wholly ghosted by what might have been; he cannot shake the proximity of Compton.

Lamar is aware of the power of his influence, but says he's not out to change the world. "The idea of me sparking change; it's got to come from within. I couldn't be saying I want Compton to change. You know, Compton is a beautiful place. You just gotta keep your eyes open."

CALIFORNIA DEMISE: TYLER, THE CREATOR AND EMA FEEL THE BAD VIBES

Village Voice **Pazz and Jop Critics Poll, 2011**

Tyler, The Creator is stuck inside "Yonkers" with those California hate-fuck blues again. Don't ask him what the matter is—you'll get an album-length spleening in response. He's rap's nouveau old-model bad boy, showing the kids that "breaking rules is cool again," rhyming impolitely about his problems with, well, everything. Many spent the year trying to gauge the murder-minded messiah MC. On *Goblin*, he came across as so ferociously indifferent, it was hard to imagine he could give a shit about anyone at all—including himself.

He's unlike all the other cool California kids of recent memory, who're writing songs that pick up where David Crosby's sailboat docked. They're obsessed with the various qualities of sand, sunshine, friendship and/or the waves, and they're too high to take a position on much else. Last year's chillwave wave was the latest iteration of California's musical posi-vibe, all bright smiles highlighted by a deep tan. Chillwave's methodology of easy hooks submerged in reverb and delay served as a constant reminder of being distant and of singers floating in their own worlds.

With decades of this cheery jangle as a cultural inheritance, it's easy to see why Tyler's Wolf Gang wants to kill 'em all, let God sort 'em out (and then kill God) or why EMA came blazing for "California" with nothing but middle fingers and lick shots for the left coast. Can you blame them? The thrill of popping that bubble is undeniable. Tyler's most (or only, depending on whom you ask) obvious talent is antagonism, a puerile needling that knows to go for the jugular—to say the exact thing you don't want to hear, flippant and cruel in equal measure. Although plenty of Californian MCs have paired rage with ridicule, Tyler's effusively macho posturing is less *Straight Outta Compton* and more like that of the man who made it his trademark: Henry Rollins. (This time around, Syd's got the 10 1/2.)

Historically, California punk has had its share of teen loathers with suicidal tendencies. Rollins is Tyler's clearest primogenitor (Eminem be damned!)—the myopic focus on bad feelings, a hangover of confused, adolescent tumult tangling hard with violent solutions. Tyler's sober indifference isolates him from the other California girls and boys, and the intensity with which he doesn't give a fuck belies just how much he actually does. It's the most un-L.A. thing he could possibly do.

So much is the same for Erika Anderson—known on-record as EMA—even though she is, in essence, Tyler's inverse. Born-and-bred Midwestern riot-grrrl rides west in search of new liberation in noise, gets grown, and explodes her heart and head open on *Past Life Martyred Saints*. It's a brute-force real-girl reveal: She's done with the archetypes and instead has an album full of blood and "20 kisses with a butterfly knife." Self-preservation is not a principal interest—she is gutting her guts and blunt about the trauma she has known instead of engaging in the apathetic yearning that typifies indie rock's notion of a "confessional." Like on *Goblin,* the volatility and capriciousness is unsettling—it makes you believe she's howling her truth.

When Anderson faces her audience, foot up on the monitor in confident, rock-star repose, and begins noosing herself with the mic cable, her methodical calm is what shocks. Her seemingly easy acquaintance with violence makes her shows seem less like performance and more like a visceral expression of how little (or much) she cares. She's a spectacular songwriter, coaxing howls from her half-stack, a tall, beautiful blonde calmly cooing, "I used to carry the gun / The gun, the gun, the gun." In the underground, she's as much of a "walking paradox" as Tyler.

Both artists goad unease for different reasons (EMA's violence is directed inward; Tyler's viciousness is often directed toward queers and women), but discomfort is crucial fuel for their spectacle. The placement of "Yonkers" and "California" in this year's poll offers evidence that listeners are taking them up on the vicarious thrill of their Cali-kid violence—regardless of whether it delights or disgusts.

WILL THE STINK OF SUCCESS RUIN THE SMELL?

LA Weekly, **February 2009**

The story of The Smell—an all-ages venue that's the wellspring for the young idea here in Los Angeles—on the surface, isn't exactly spectacular. Like most clubs, it's a depot of questionable haircuts and bombastic bands. Yet, The Smell is different than the rest: it's a no-booze, not-for-profit operation that is staffed most entirely by teenage volunteers. The recent success of some of the exciting bands it fostered—namely No Age—has made The Smell a point of focus for the worldwide underground, a place delivering on punk's unfulfilled promises of DIY community and inclusion.

***

The way people talk about Jim Smith, you'd think he was sanctified and risen. The story of every Smell band, every volunteer's gee-whiz excitement, always hinges on Smith, who opened the venue eleven years ago. A labor union organizer by day and dutiful scene facilitator by night, Smith is taciturn and humble. He's got an old fashioned gallantry to him; he dresses in working man's clothes and decries little. He has the gravitas of a man living by a code. Smith closes up at The Smell at 1 or 2 a.m. then goes to work at 6 a.m., night after night. Without complaint or even the slightest sense that this unpaid toil brings him anything other than gratification.

If Smith is The Smell's heart, No Age are its arteries. The story of L.A.'s zeitgeist, noise-pop duo is braided with the venue's genesis. Given the amount of press and hype the band has garnered in the last year and a half, it's become part of their mythic tale: The Smell as the house No Age built. This is objectively true; talking to guitarist Randy Randall in early October, he lamented that though he and drummer Dean Spunt helped break concrete for the construction of The Smell's second bathroom, No Age was on tour during its completion.

No Age might very well be the coolest band in America right now, and it's easy to understand why. Being a No Age fan feels like more than mere fandom, which is fitting since No Age feel like more than just another band. They stand for hope and big ideas as well as simple ones: have fun, include everyone, be positive, do good work. It's an active rejection of adult cynicism. You could call it anti-capitalist, but there's no indication anyone involved has given it that much thought. These are the same principals that The Smell seems to impart on everyone who passes through its piss-soaked doorway.

***

In No Age's Dean Spunt and Randy Randall, Jim Smith found his two most dedicated and willing volunteers—true sons of the scene. Like most of the kids who've found purchase in The Smell's hallowed space, they were refugees from the city's rock club circuit. "One of the first places I ever played was the Cobalt Cafe, in the Valley," says Spunt. "They'd do a bill of six local bands and when you walked in they asked you what band you were there to see. Once you got over 50 people for your band, which was impossible, then you got 50 bucks and a dollar a head after that." He adds, "They made you really feel like a kid." Never mind that he still was one.

"The first time playing Smell, it was the anti-version of that." No booze. No tickets. No backstage. No bullshit. No security hassling you. No pay to play. The Smell is the very definition of anti-club. "At The Smell you were treated as an equal," explains Smith. "The kids that come, they are people, not 'patrons.'"

When Spunt and Randall discovered The Smell in 1998, it wasn't the province of teen punks, but a dingy downtown venue that'd been colonized by the experimental noise scene—Nels Cline and Win Records bands. The two promptly began booking shows for their then-band, Wives, and as Spunt puts it "we took the place over." They began booking hardcore and punk bills, including an all-female crust band from the Valley, Dead Banana Ladies, who would soon become scene-queens Mika Miko. Exit old noise dudes, hello excitable tenth graders of the Inland Empire.

Spunt's devotion was instant: "The first time I went there I thought 'I want to be here every day!' and until about a year, year and a half ago, I was. I was there every day. It was so crazy and so special."

Spunt and Randall joined the cabal of people around Smith who were deeply involved in keeping the place open. In 2002, after the Great White club-fire tragedy in Providence, The Smell, like many on-the-fringe-of-legit spaces around the country, was closed by the fire marshal. For the next six months the Smell crew worked to bring the club up to code as quickly as possible. Spunt moved all the shows that had already been booked into a squat where he was living in Hollywood. Almost nightly, there was a four-band bill in his living room, and almost every day the two would be down at The Smell, putting on new doors, building and painting, alongside Smith and the rest of the regulars.

Amid the process, The Smell became more than a hangout, it became a place Spunt and Randall were responsible for keeping running. "Anthony Berryman from Soddamn Inssein came down to the video store where I worked," explains Randall. "He told me 'Jim cannot do this by himself. Listen, you are going to get keys. I don't want to hear that you are flaking on shows you booked or not showing up.' I had to learn how to do sound, how to put the mics up there and run the soundboard, be there every night. Jim would try and pay me, and I would avoid him. He'd try to slip a twenty in your pocket somehow."

"And then we did the same thing to Mika Miko, because Wives were going on tour for four months. They were there everyday and playing twice a week," says Spunt.

In the years since The Smell's re-birth, the venue's stakeholders have gone from being just a trusted few bands and regulars to the scene at large. The door was thrown open for everyone to get involved, and it wasn't simply an issue of good intentions. No Age began to tour frequently (sometimes with Smith in tow), as did Mika Miko, Abe Vigoda and longtime Smell booker/compatriot Brian Miller. Randall explains, "Jim figured that it had to get bigger than just us and other bands, it had to be the kids, too." He made a "What Would Jim Do" book that volunteers consult; a dozen volunteers have keys. The Smell transitioned from the hands of a few to any and all willing hands.

"[Jim] really sent it out to the community, that they *have to* do it," says Randall. "People complain that The Smell won't book their band, but then you have to ask them, 'Well, how many shows have you been to? Have you volunteered there?' It's about nurturing the community."

***

Backstage after No Age's show in London in late October, a young blogger has been waiting, impatiently, for the 30 minutes since Spunt and Randall got offstage, to interview them for her website. They are soggy and winded from their set and trying to get it together to walk across the street to play a second, "secret" show for 120 die-hards at a 90-capacity sushi bar. Despite the fact that the girl is openly resentful and has a list of 40 terrible questions, they indulge her. With smiles. They are unwaveringly polite. It is the California way to never offend anyone, but their gentleness, removed from the context of The Smell's downtown alley, becomes immediately recognizable as the spirit of Jim Smith. After 10 minutes, they have to go. They invite her along—she carries the cymbal stands.

At the packed sushi joint, kids are blowing up balloons, and Smell-scenester Vice Cooler is deejaying R. Kelly too loud. The band heads backstage—a stairwell to the roof—where they learn the Misfits' classic "Where Eagles Dare." Someone had dialed up the guitar-tab on their iPhone, learned it and proofed it against the collective memory of the band's friends that have gathered in the stairwell. Five minutes later, Spunt and Randall open their set with it. Ebullient fans scream along: "I AIN'T NO GODDAMN SON OF A BITCH! YOU BETTER THINK ABOUT IT BAY-BAY!" The floor begins to flex wildly under the pogoing people, so, at the behest of Randall, the audience sits down, which sparks a pig-pile pit. The band blazes through a short set with everyone rolling on each other, singing along and writhing on the floor.

At the club show No Age played just an hour before, for 1,200 composed Londoners, they were great—a truly fun band. But to see them play a party at this too-small spot, heavy with die-hards, is to see No Age at their incandescent, miracle-band best. It is then that you get that they are so much more than a band. To so many, they are deliverance, they are everything everyone says they are—everything we've wished and waited for in punk.

Since its inception 30-odd years ago, punk has had a spotty history of living up to its best intentions, which is part of its charm. Periodically, there have been bands—most notably Crass, Fugazi, Bad Brains, The Ex, Bikini Kill—or labels (K, Dischord) or scenes that sprang up with radical notions that inspired a paradigm shift. It is a matter of inspiration—and great records or live shows are necessary to back it up, to wrap people up in the big ideas—the pugnacious do-it-yourself dogma is transmogrified into something urbane and empowering. It's a rare sort of once-or-twice-a-decade thing, when a band shows us we can be more than fans, and that this can be about something other than entertainment, getting wasted or getting laid. It is an alchemical shift, where music becomes exactly what you believed it was when your heart was 15 and pure, and all the hope and time you've given it pays out. The Smell is home to one of these coalescent moments, No Age is one of these bands.

***

While The Smell may have indoctrinated No Age on how to approach their career and given them an ideological toehold for their music, it didn't necessarily prepare them for success. The band is being held up as an emblem of positivity in the media, hailed as a signal of a new Los Angeles, and the band is wearing the weight of those expectations. "We want to play and do our thing but the visibility puts a lot of stress on people around us, the community of L.A.," says Spunt. "I have to wonder, like, did we fuck something up?" What happens in a scene of equals when suddenly one band is declared king?

***

It's the morning after what should have been No Age's triumphant return to The Smell. It's been a big year for the boys; their debut on Sub Pop, Nouns, has the underground hyperventilating with glee, and has brought them to the attention of the overground: they have been profiled in *The New Yorker* and played on a late night chat show. They have been nominated for a Grammy for their album packaging. After months of non-stop touring, they had almost two weeks home for a break, and booked a hush-hush show at The Smell. The show was moderately attended, but the audience had few familiar faces. Then, after the third song, in a pocket of strange silence, a kid yelled giddily from where the pit should have been, "YOU WERE ON MTV!" Dean and Randy exchanged glances and Dean quickly counted off into the next 4/4 blitzkrieg; a handful of kids pogo, while the rest gawk silently at the band.

No Age shows here, historically, have been a crush of sweat and scream-alongs. The show had a curious pall for a band that has enjoyed such a fast ride to fame, and it exacts a toll from the already-exhausted boys. Randy explains, "What was weird last night was that we were in our home, but there were a bunch of strangers in it. Normally we might yell out to our friends in the audience, but there were so many strange faces."

"It was just weird. It was The Smell, but it wasn't," says Spunt. "Me and Randy were pretty much just hanging alone. It was fine, it was cool, but it wasn't our friends. I wasn't concerned with [the] amount of people. It was just... All of our friends were busy—Mika Miko was playing a show, Abe Vigoda was doing stuff, everybody is doing stuff on a bigger level, so..." He trails off. As the No Age's profile has risen, so has that of some other Smell bands, namely Mika Miko and Abe Vigoda. Lately, the press has portrayed both bands as No Age's retinue rather than the close-knit cabal they are.

"After last night, I was bummed. This morning I was trying to get clarity on it and I cried. It's not that I've lost my friends—but doing this was fun because we were doing it all together," Randall confides. "Being gone so much, you miss the parties, you miss birthdays, and then after a while I'm not expected to be there, so no one is bummed when you don't show up. I have lost certain community ties, friends." He continues, "Last night I was thinking, 'What makes you think you can just come home and expect everyone to show up?' Who am I to ask for that when I am not there?" He sighs, "The reason I cried was the sacrifices. There's been too many. Too many little things that I didn't know were on the line."

It is Jim Smith, more than anyone, who insists that all the attention on No Age and The Smell is not having a corrosive effect. Despite what naysayers may predict, The Smell isn't losing its vortical tension. While a lot of the regulars insist that shows regularly sell out now—which would have been a freak occurrence in the past— Smith is reluctant to cop to any discernible shift, in attendance or otherwise. "Sure, The Smell is in transition," he says, "but it's always been that way, since the beginning—evolving and growing. Fundamentally, nothing is different. We still operate on the principles by which it was founded. The energy is still there. We have remained intact."

DISPATCHES FROM THE DESERT: COACHELLA

Chicago Reader, **May 2005**

As soon as my friend and I got out of the car to begin our mile-and-a-half-long walk from "Coachella: The Parking Lot" to "Coachella: The Music Festival in the Desert" a couple weekends ago, I could hear them, faint but instantly recognizable and uniquely heart-warming to a girl of a certain age: Ponies. Ponies neighing. Coachella kicks it upscale—instead of spreading out a zillion-band lineup on the sticky blacktop of a sports-arena parking lot, the fest rents 78 acres of manicured fields from the Empire Polo Club in Indio, California. And before you get to the bands, or even to the long snaky line for the sun-ripened Port-O-Lets, you walk past the barns and corrals that house the scene's year-round residents. When I got there, they were stamping and saying hello to a few of the roughly 96,000 people who'd come to pass out face down in the grass, relive their goth teenhood, and/or see the Arcade Fire.

The line for admittance, even for press, was half an hour long. I immediately lost track of my friend and wound up tagging along with Kelefa Sanneh, a pop critic for *The New York Times*. Once inside the festival grounds, we started making our rounds like dutiful interns, visiting the main stage, the side stage, and the three performance tents—Gobi, Sahara and Mojave. Our conversations went like this:

Me: "What band is this?"

K: "The Raveonettes" / "Snow Patrol" / "Eisley."

Me: "Really? They're awful."

K: Makes razor-sharp joke referencing the band's audience, influences or publicist.

(Repeat for three hours.)

I noticed that Kelefa was barely taking notes on the groups we were watching, and because I didn't want to look like a fastidious cub reporter by comparison, I only pulled out my own notebook once all afternoon. When I opened it again to remind myself what I'd been inspired to write down, all I found was "Jamie Cullum: piano = awful."

I decided to skip U.K. hype victims Razorlight, since I felt like I already knew everything I wanted to about them—sitting behind me on the flight from Chicago, they'd spent the entire time talking loudly about how fucked-up they'd gotten at such and such a party and which extremely famous persons they'd been hanging out with. Instead I went to the VIP area, where I saw the very-sweaty editors of several major American entertainment magazines shaking hands with the bassist from Snow Patrol. Then I overheard a couple of them trying to decide which one of the two black dudes wandering around the tent was the black dude from Bloc Party.

Around 7 p.m., just as Wilco was starting up, the sun began to set over the mountains that surround the Coachella Valley. Maybe people just needed a rest after spending hours cooking in the desert sun or getting sloppy with the mamis in the beer tent, but it seemed like everyone was prone on the grass, taking in the scenery. Wilco's breezy sound, trilling Hammond organ, and soft-thrill solos turned out to pair well with sunsets and swaying palm trees—I felt the majestic rightness of it in a sudden easy swell, my first "Ahhh...Coachella" moment of the weekend.

Biplanes circled in the purpling sky, towing banners reading "NEW GORILLAZ ALBUM OUT MAY 24" or "SIRIUS (heart)s WEEZER." That was the only way they could deliver those messages—the festival's promoter, Goldenvoice, refrains from slutting the audience out to corporate sponsors. More than anything, this is what separates Coachella from major U.S. festivals like Warped, Ozzfest and Lollapalooza: no Yoo-hoo truck, no free Slim Jims, no Army recruiters, no 20-foot inflatable women doubling as water slides. The relatively few booths were far from the stages, and most were pushing stuff at least tangentially related to the main event (music magazines, silkscreened concert posters). The only vendors you could find near the main stage were selling churros and lemonade.

After sunset, three-story TV screens flickered to life on either side of the main stage, each displaying a rotating Weezer logo. It looked like almost everybody at the festival had crowded around the stage, and they were screaming—nay, roaring—for the band. I watched Weezer do "Undone - the Sweater song" from the bathroom line in the press section of the backstage area, three quarters of a mile away.

Wandering the grounds, I had a hard time crediting Coachella with being America's only European-style festival, as it's often described; instead, the nobody-asked-for-it eclecticism of the many small attractions called up the ghost of Lollapaloozas past. (It was also pretty much guaranteed to be lost on folks who'd driven across six states to see Coldplay.) A quick sampling of the random crap on offer: 50 garbage cans decorated in outsider-art style, a DIY playzone with a bike-powered merry-go-round, a "chill-out tent" with giant misting fans and a soundtrack of the sort of lite house you hear in the dressing rooms at Express, and a wacky-hippie amusement consisting of a large metal sculpture and an armload of mallets. Lower-tier bookings, especially club acts, played to mostly-empty tents whenever the headliners were on. The outdoor film screenings drew similarly sad crowds—maybe two people were watching the Minutemen movie, *We Jam Econo*, at 11:30 p.m.

Like the Pixies last year and the Stooges the year before, Bauhaus was the big story at Coachella. Gossip about the band circulated like currency among the band's fans: that Peter Murphy is now a Sufi Muslim and lives in a village five hours from Istanbul, or that the other members of the band, though they all live in Southern California, hadn't played together since the 1998 reunion tour and only decided to when Coachella offered them a giant pile of cash. (Based on what the other big names got paid, it had to be well into six figures—the ticket money really adds up at $150 a pop for a weekend pass.) Bauhaus had wanted to release 50 bats during their set but abandoned the plan, provoking an unfounded rumor that the city of Indio had intervened by stretching an ordinance that forbids bird releases at night.

I was never goth. I've never liked Bauhaus enough to own one of their records; that said, the band's performance at Coachella was unfuckingbelievable. They hit the stage obscured by fog and white light and struck up the descending bass line and graveyard rattle of "Bela Lugosi's Dead," and everyone was craning their necks because you could hear Peter Murphy, but not see him. He finally entered stage left, suspended upside down eight feet off the ground with his arms folded like bat's wings, being towed slowly sideways toward center stage on almost invisible cables and crooning, "Undead undead undead." It wasn't until Murphy had been pulled back offstage, still upside down, and returned on foot that I first noticed his outfit, which was probably astronomically-expensive designer stuff but looked like '70s ski pants and a top from Jacques Cousteau's club-wear line. He gave up the zillion-watt drama nonstop, brandishing a long staff that looked like a martial-arts weapon—he slung it around for emphasis and almost took out bassist David J twice. Whatever Coachella paid these guys to reunite, it was worth it.

Still, Bauhaus wasn't all I'd come to see, so mid-set I raced back to the side stage and caught the end of Mercury Rev's epic space-rock blast. They were dressed like pirates, if pirates could order from International Male—lacy women's blouses are the new look for dudes in bands this season. Spoon was up next, and doled out terse, gorgeously ragged versions of both old and new songs for an impressive crowd. Between tunes you could hear Chris Martin of Coldplay—at that moment headlining the main stage—rhapsodizing about the band's new record to the 70,000-deep crowd, suggesting that it might be the greatest album of all time. I took this as my cue to call it a night.

I didn't make it back out to the festival till 4 p.m. on Sunday, but of the 16 bands I missed, I'd seen half of them recently and hadn't heard of the other half. I checked out the Fiery Furnaces for two songs and then managed to get within 30 feet of the Gobi tent for M.I.A.—the only act I saw do an encore all weekend. In fact, there might've been a minor civil disturbance if Ms. Arulpragasam hadn't come back on for another few minutes of her Neneh Cherry-goes-favela-funk bassplosion—clearly she shouldn't have been stuck in the littlest tent, which was kind of like a 500-capacity yurt. I ate some more churros, caught Tegan and Sara's hit song, then sat in the shade and ignored The Futureheads from a half mile away.

A friend commandeered a VIP golf-cart transport by convincing the driver that he was in Bright Eyes, and we sped across the grounds in hopes of making it to the Arcade Fire's side-stage set. The entire back side of the stage was 30 or 40 people deep with members of other bands, and out front the audience was as huge and ebullient as it'd been for Weezer. Trent Reznor whizzed past us on another golf cart, a girl tucked under each arm.

Sunday's sunset slot belonged to the reunited Gang of Four. I almost didn't watch, afraid that my teen-years favorite might suck. The guys in Gang of Four are nearly as old as my parents, but took the stage spry and lively and jumped immediately into "Damaged Goods"—a song that is, more than a quarter century later, the template for dance punk as we know it. Frontman Jon King threw himself around the stage in a slate-gray suit, wild-eyed and vitriolic, spitting "Sometimes I'm thinking that I love you / But I know it's only lust" as Andy Gill's guitar slashed—and then, when the frenzied final choruses stopped and switched to the outro, bassist Dave Allen flubbed it, not only playing through the pause but continuing to play the wrong part. The rest of the band glared at him. And he kept fucking up—by halfway through the fourth song I was disgusted with him. His subpar playing was forcing Gang of Four to fake their way to the ends of the tunes, band-practice style, in front of 50,000 people. I left too early to catch the set closer, but it was in a local paper, the *Desert Sun*, the next day: King destroyed a microwave with a baseball bat.

I went to see Aesop Rock on the side stage, and with Mr. Lif as hype man he was better than usual—an audience of a few thousand yelled "Life is a bitch" along with him. The wind picked up, bringing in the aroma of the Port-O-Let villages. By the time Nine Inch Nails took the main stage it felt like a sandstorm was in the making, and I was headed back toward the parking lot. I turned and saw, a mile away, Trent Reznor's snarling head, as big as a house on the Jumbotrons and framed by illuminated palm trees. Over the distant din, I heard ponies.

PART FIVE

FAITH

THE PASSION OF DAVID BAZAN

Chicago Reader, **July 2009**

"People used to compare him to Jesus," says a backstage manager as David Bazan walks offstage, guitar in hand. "But not so much anymore."

It's Thursday, July 2, and Bazan has just finished his set at Cornerstone, the annual Christian music festival held on a farm near Bushnell, Illinois. He hasn't betrayed his crowd the way Dylan did when he went electric—this is something very different. The kids filling the 1,500-capacity tent know their Jesus from their Judas. There was a time when Bazan's fans believed he was speaking, or rather singing, the Word. Not so much anymore.

As front man for Pedro the Lion, the band he led from 1995 till 2005, Bazan was Christian indie rock's first big crossover star, predating Sufjan by nearly a decade and paving the way for the music's success outside the praise circuit. But as he straddled the secular and spiritual worlds, Bazan began to struggle with his faith. Unable to banish from his mind the possibility that the God he'd loved and prayed to his whole life didn't exist, he started drinking heavily. In '05, the last time he played Cornerstone, he was booted off the grounds for being shit-faced, a milk jug full of vodka in his hand. (The festival is officially dry.)

I worked as Bazan's publicist from 2000 till 2004. When I ran into him in April—we were on a panel together at the Calvin College Festival of Faith & Music in Grand Rapids—I hadn't seen him or talked to him in five and a half years. The first thing he said to me was, "I'm not sure if you know this, but my relationship with Christ has changed pretty dramatically in the last few years."

He went on to explain that since 2004 he's been flitting between atheist, skeptic and agnostic, and that lately he's hovering around agnostic—he can't flat-out deny the presence of God in the world, but Bazan doesn't exactly believe in him, either.

Pedro the Lion won a lot of secular fans in part because Bazan's lyrics—incisive examinations of faith, set to fuzzed-out guitar hooks—

have a through-a-glass-darkly quality, acknowledging the imperfection of human understanding rather than insisting on an absolute truth. As the post-9/11 culture wars began to heat up, Pedro the Lion albums took a turn toward the parabolic: an outraged Bazan churned out artful songs about what befalls the righteous and the folly of those who believe God is on their side.

Bazan's relationship with the divine started out pretty uncomplicated, though. Raised outside Seattle in the Pentecostal church where his father was the music director, he hewed closely to Christian orthodoxy, attended Bible college, and married at 23. Now 33, he didn't do a lot of thinking about politics until the 1999 WTO protests. "Growing up, Christianity didn't feel oppressive for the most part, because it was filtered through my parents. They were and are so sincere, and I saw in them a really pure expression of unconditional love and service," he says. "Once I stepped away, I could see the oppression of it."

Bazan's *Curse Your Branches*, due September 1 on Barsuk, is a visceral accounting of what happened after that. It's a harrowing breakup record—except he's dumping God, Jesus and the evangelical life. It's his first full-length solo album and also his most autobiographical effort: its drunken narratives, spasms of spiritual dissonance, and family tensions are all scenes from the recent past.

Bazan says he tried to Band-Aid his loss of faith and the painful end of Pedro the Lion with about 18 months of "intense" drinking. "If I didn't have responsibilities, if I wasn't watching [my daughter] Ellanor, I had a deep drive to get blacked out," he says. But as he made peace with where he found himself, the compulsion to get obliterated began to wane. On *Curse Your Branches*, Bazan sometimes directs the blame and indignation at himself, other times at Jesus and the faith. He's mourning what he's lost, and he knows there's no going back.

"All fallen leaves should curse their branches / For not letting them decide where they should fall / And not letting them refuse to fall at all," he sings on the title track, with more than a touch of fuck-you in his voice. On "When We Fell," backed by a galloping beat and Wilson-boys harmonies, he calls faith a curse put on him by God: "If my mother cries when I tell her what I discovered / Then I hope she remembers she told me to follow my heart / And if you bully her like you've done me with fear of damnation / Then I hope she can see you for what you are."

The album closer, "In Stitches," may be the best song Bazan's ever written. It's the most emotionally bare piece on the album, and works as a synopsis of the story:

This brown liquor wets my tongue
My fingers find the stitches
Firmly back and forth they run
I need no other memory
Of the bits of me I left
When all this lethal drinking
Is hopefully to forget
About you

He follows it with an even more devastating verse, confessing that his efforts to erase God have failed:

I might as well admit it
Like I've even got a choice
The crew have killed the captain
But they still can hear his voice
A shadow on the water
A whisper in the wind
On long walks my with daughter
Who is lately full of questions
About you
About you

The second "about you" comes in late, in a strong falsetto, and those two words carry his entire burden—the anger, desire, confusion and grief.

Since the jug-of-vodka incident, Bazan has kept a pretty low profile, doing a couple of modest solo tours and releasing an EP of raw-sounding songs on Barsuk. Pedro the Lion was a reliable paycheck—most of its albums sold in the neighborhood of 50,000 copies, and the group toured regularly, drawing 400 to 600 people a night. His most recent tour couldn't have been more different: Bazan doesn't have a road band put together yet for his solo stuff, but he couldn't afford to wait for *Curse Your Branches* to come out. So he found another way to keep in touch with his most devoted fans, booking 60 solo shows in houses and other noncommercial spaces. He played intimate acoustic sets to maybe 40 people each night, at $20 a ticket, and took questions between songs—some of them, unsurprisingly, about the tough spiritual questions his new material raises.

Despite his outspokenness on those questions, he was invited back to Cornerstone for the first time this year.

"I know David has a long history of being a seeker and trying to navigate through his faith. Cornerstone is open to that," says John Herrin, the festival's director. "We welcome plenty of musicians who may not identify themselves as Christians but are artists with an ongoing connection to faith.... We're glad to have him back. We don't give up on people; we don't give up on the kids here who are seeking, trying to figure out what they don't believe and what they do. This festival was built on patience."

At Cornerstone, where I catch up with him behind the fair-food midway, Bazan laughs when I suggest that he's there trying to save the Christians. "I am. I am really invested, because I came up in it and I love a lot of evangelical Christians—I care what happens with the movement," he says. "The last 30 years of it have been hijacked; the boomer evangelicals, they were seduced in the most embarrassing and scandalous way into a social, political and economical posture that is the antithesis of Jesus' teaching."

With *Curse Your Branches* and in his recent shows, he's inverting the usual call to witness: "You might be the only Christian they ever meet." He's the doubter's witness, and he might be the only agnostic these Christian kids ever really listen to.

When I talk to some of those kids in the merch tent the day after Bazan's set, many of them seem to be trying to spin the new songs, straining to categorize them as Christian so they can justify continuing to listen to them. One fan says it's good that Bazan is singing about the perils of sin, "particularly sexual sin." Another interprets the songs as a witness of addiction, the testimony of the stumbling man.

Cultural critic and progressive Christian author David Dark, who since 2003 has become one of Bazan's closest friends, claims that Bazan's skepticism and anger are in-line with biblical tradition. "I doubt this is what your average Cornerstone attendee means, but when David is addressing his idea of his God, the one that he fears exists but refuses to believe in, when he is telling God, 'If this is the situation with us and you, then fuck you—the people who love you, I hope they see you for who you are,' when he's doing that, he is at his most biblical. If we are referring to the deep strains of complaint and prayers and tirades against conceptions of God in the Bible— yes, then in that way he's in your Christian tradition. But I disagree that he's an advocate *for* the biblical."

When I tell Bazan that there are kids at Cornerstone resisting the clear message of his songs, he's surprised. "That someone could listen to what I was saying and think that I was saying it apologetically—like, in a way that characterizes [doubt] as the wrong posture—bums me out, but that's pretty high-concept given how I'm presenting this stuff. So I have to hand it to someone who can keep on spinning what is so clearly something else." He pauses for a long moment, then adds, "I don't want to be that misunderstood."

During the two days I follow Bazan and his fans around the Cornerstone campus, though, it becomes clear that he isn't really misunderstood at all. Everyone knows what he's singing about—what's happening is that his listeners are taking great pains to sidestep the obvious. "Well, his songs have always been controversial," one says, but when asked to pinpoint the source of the controversy suggests it's because he swears—nothing about not believing in hell or not taking the Bible as God's word. Bazan's agnosticism is the elephant in the merch tent.

Fans rhapsodize about Bazan's work: they love his honesty, they love how they can relate to him, how he's not proselytizing, how he's speaking truth—but they don't tend to delve into what exactly that truth might be. Brice Evans, a 24-year-old from Harrisburg, Illinois, who came to Cornerstone specifically to see Bazan's set, dances artfully around it. "He's showing a side of Christianity that no other band shows," Evans says. "He's trying to get a message across that's more than that."

It's hard to say if anybody is conscious of the irony: the "side of Christianity" Bazan sings about is disenfranchisement from it.

"I think with *Curse Your Branches* David expands the space of the talk-about-able," says Dark. "It's not confessional in the sense that he's down on himself and trying to confess something to God in hopes of being forgiven. I think that's what crowds are trying to make of him, but they're going to have a tougher time when they get the record."

Bazan is known for his dialogues with fans, and during his set he's affable, taking questions from the crowd. Tonight's audience, openly anxious and awed, keeps it light at first: "Would you rather be a werewolf or a vampire?" Then he opens with the new album's lead track, "Hard to Be," a sobering song with an especially hard-hitting second verse:

Wait just a minute
You expect me to believe
That all this misbehaving
Grew from one enchanted tree?
And helpless to fight it
We should all be satisfied
With this magical explanation
For why the living die
And why it's hard to be
Hard to be, hard to be
A decent human being?

By the time he finishes those lines I can see half a dozen people crying; a woman near me is trembling and sobbing. Others have their heads in their hands. Many look stunned, but no one leaves. When the song ends, the applause is thunderous.

After Bazan plays a cover of Leonard Cohen's "Hallelujah," reinstating the sacrilegious verses left out of the best-known versions, someone shouts, "How's your soul?" Bazan looks up from tuning his guitar and says, "My soul? Oh, it's fine." This elicits an "Amen, brother!" from the back of the tent.

Following Bazan's set, a throng of fans—kids, young women with babies on their hips, a handful of youth pastors—queues up around the side of the stage to talk to him. Some kids want hugs and ask geeked-out questions, but just as many attempt to feel him out in a sly way. "I really wished you had played 'Lullaby,'" says one kid, naming a very early Pedro the Lion song that's probably the most worshipful in Bazan's catalog. A few gently bait him, referring to Scripture the way gang members throw signs, eager for a response that will reveal where Bazan is really at.

During discussions like this Bazan doesn't usually get into the subtle barometric fluctuations in his relationship with Jesus, but that still leaves room for plenty of post-show theological talk. "This process feels necessary and natural for these people," he says. "They're in a precarious situation—maybe I am, too. To maintain their particular posture, they have to figure out: Do they need to get distance from me, or is it just safe enough to listen to? I empathize as people are trying to gauge, 'Is this guy an atheist? Because I heard he was.'"

Bazan has chosen sides, but old ideas linger. "Some time ago, we were discussing [the Pedro the Lion song] 'Foregone Conclusions,'" Dark says. "I told him I was impressed with the lines 'You were too busy steering conversation toward the Lord / To hear the voice of the Spirit / Begging you to shut the fuck up / You thought it must be the devil / Trying to make you go astray / Besides it could not have been the Lord / Because you don't believe He talks that way.' I thought, what a liberating word for people who've been shoved around by all manner of brainwash. But also, Dave's doing something even more subtle, as many interpret the unforgivable sin to be blasphemy against the Holy Spirit—confusing the voice of God for the voice of the devil—so there's a whole 'nother level of theological devastation going on in the song.

"When I brought it up, he laughed and told me he still worries about going to hell for that one. He knows that it's horribly funny that he feels that way, but he won't lie by saying he's entirely over it. He's both 100 percent sincere and 100 percent ironically detached. He's haunted even as he pushes forward, saying what he feels even though he half fears doing so will be cosmically costly for him."

After a long few years in the wilderness, Bazan seems happy—though he's still parsing out his beliefs, he's visibly relieved to be out and open about where he's *not* at. "It's more comfortable for me to be agnostic," he says. "There's less internal tension by far—that's even with me duking it out with my perception of who God is on a pretty regular basis, and having a lot of uncertainty on that level. For now, just being is enough. Whether things happen naturally, completely outside an author, or whether the dynamics of earth and people are that way because God created them—or however you want to credit it—if you look around and pay attention and observe, there is enough right here to know how to act, to know how to live, to be at peace with one another.

"Because I grew up believing in hell and reckoning, there is a voice in me that says, 'That might not cut it with the man upstairs,' but I think that that has to be enough. For me it is enough."

FLIRTING WITH RELIGION: RICKIE LEE JONES

Chicago Reader, **March 2007**

Contemporary praise pop may posit Jesus as a personal savior, but much of the language it uses is a sort of salvation jargon that hardly speaks to the uninitiated—and it tends to frame worship as something done at a remove, with we sinners here on Earth and God distant in Heaven. The songs on Rickie Lee Jones' new *Sermon on Exposition Boulevard* (New West), on the other hand, have all the hallmarks of love songs—the lust and the longing, the desperation and solitude, the new love raising its defiant head, the wounded heart healed. But these love songs are about something far less tangible than romance: they're songs of faith. It's as if Jones has divorced the secular world and her rebound boyfriend is Jesus Christ.

Jones improvised the bulk of the lyrics for the album's 13 songs while the tape was rolling. She riffed on *The Words*, a book published by her friend Lee Cantelon that removes the words of Jesus from their biblical context and arranges them by topic—a kind of Cliffs Notes to the New Testament. The record starts easy enough, with the sleepy jangle of "Nobody Knows My Name," over which Jones—her voice still the sinewy, reedy cry muscled into insistent girl-soul that we recognize from back in '79—sings of a God present in things both elemental and man-made, an everywhere-at-once spirit, moving freely, unknown and unrecognized. It's a lament of faith in a faithless world, but it also establishes a theme that recurs throughout *Sermon*: that Jesus and belief in Jesus have been co-opted and codified by The Religious Right, who set rigid parameters for who can worship and how. They narrowly define what a relationship with God can look like: Jesus is in the church, on the cross, on the side of the good and the righteous. Jones returns to us the gnostic Jesus, the people's savior, who's down with everyone and everything, not just the pious spittin' heavy hosannas between the pews.

Most of *Sermon* is in first person, but the songs aren't personal testaments of belief per se. On the second track, "Gethsemane," she sings a sort of internal monologue, imagining Jesus' foxhole-pleading with his father as he awaits his fate. The first few times I heard it, I thought it was baby-please-take-me-back post-breakup desperation: "You wake up one morning and you're by yourself / You're on your own," Jones sings, and later, "All I want is your hand." Christ's willing obedience to God's plan is the very model of faith, but Jones cleaves it with a tender lick of humanity. Her portrait of Jesus is much more casual than the one you get from cracking a hymnal.

The most remarkable thing about the record isn't Jones' recasting of Jesus but the way she transmits her own faith: it's a soft sell, relying on the beauty and aliveness of her message rather than heavy-handed threats of fire and brimstone. Underneath the metaphors and the transmuted bits of the Gospel of Luke that pass for a chorus is the true light of the record, Jones' own eureka moment, a tiny thing laid carefully in each song. You get the sense that therein lies her hope for the world—a hope not of universal conversion but of peace and salvation for all. It'd sound insufferably New Agey and annoying if Rickie weren't our West Coast, California-cooled Patti, who fell hard for jazz instead of rock 'n' roll and preferred her own diary-poems to Rimbaud's. Both ecstatic and world-weary, she sings of the "soft-shoed devil" in "Circle in the Sand" as though they're well acquainted, like the devil might be a local bad boy she knows from back in her wild-girl days.

Last Saturday night, when Jones came through town, her wild-girl days seemed far behind her. She blew in from the blizzard and walked up the theater aisle directly onto the stage, her scarf and coat still on, a to-go coffee cup in her hand. She pulled out the piano bench, dropped her outside clothes in a pile on the floor, pushed up her shirtsleeves, and sat down to get to work. She was wearing lace-up shoes, a sweatshirt, no makeup, and cargo pants with a bunch of stuff in the pockets—she looked like this was just a stop she had to make on her way to Petco for some litter. But then, in the quick silence between the end of a song and the start of the applause, someone yelled "Rickie!" She looked up from under her long blond tangles and flashed a huge, knowing smile, and in that moment she was all rock star.

For the first few songs of the set it was just Jones at the piano. She gave some forgotten cuts the once-over, seeming purposeful and confident and comfortable with her dominion over the music and the crowd. After "The Last Chance Texaco," she was joined by her six-piece backing band, most of which appears on *Sermon*—and which included Cantelon himself, doing backup incantations. They ambled through almost the entire album, their churning, fuzzed-out tangle recalling the Velvet Underground rather than the sometimes adult-contemporary sound of the studio recording. Jones strapped on an electric guitar and occasionally did double duty as a shaman: Her voice shrank and expanded, at one extreme tiny enough to be mistaken for a child's, at the other clarion and full. She let loose whispers, holy howls, and even a swampy Waits-ian growl on "Tried to Be a Man."

The songs meandered and circled back on themselves, picking up and shedding new instrumental layers as they went and almost never doing the same thing twice—sometimes they threatened to get away from the band entirely. But Jones was the real show. She nearly yelled the words to "It Hurts," giving voice to the loneliness of the A.D. world—"It hurts / To be here / When you're gone." The song could be a love letter from Mary Magdalene to an absent Jesus or a prayer from a disappointed disciple. "My only precious thing I had / Has been broken." But as electric guitar arced and receded and furious strumming and choral ahhhs welled up around Jones, as she squeezed her eyes shut and bent in half, pulling the mic down with her, as her agony turned to ecstasy and her accusing wail turned triumphant, it became clear what we were hearing—it was a redemption song.

WHY MICHAEL JACKSON'S PAST MIGHT BE GARY, INDIANA'S ONLY FUTURE

Village Voice, **July 2009**

The first thing I noticed was that Michael Jackson was gone. Downtown Gary, Indiana's main drag hosted a wide-scale mural project in 2002, fantastic possible futures for the city's boarded-up buildings painted directly onto the boards, with an MJ adorning the old record store, symbolically turning his back on Gary, three digits of his bejeweled glove-hand blotted out with graffiti, as if he were giving his birthplace the finger. It was an odd touch of realism amid the mis-scaled office scenes of ferns and giant computers; Michael had been painted with care and detail. Now, much of downtown has been re-boarded, and he has disappeared again.

I'd been driving from downstate all day, with news reports of his death getting more and more detailed as time passed. Shortly after arriving home, a friend texted what I was already thinking: "We should go to Gary." Hitting one of Chicago's impromptu MJ-tribute nights didn't seem right—*Thriller* had taught me what it meant to have music be your whole life, to be a devoted fan; *Thriller* was the first album that was all mine, not my parents'—and so, a vigil seemed more appropriate than a dance party. Gary is where it began, and it was only 33 miles from my house. The toll booths on I-90 West pumped *Off the Wall* in every lane.

The Jackson family home is about a mile off an unlit freeway exit. You pass the bank, the only one in town. When I did a travel piece on Gary a few years ago for the *Chicago Reader*, people were quick to brag about how things were looking up: They had a bank again, after several years without one. Its gleam stands in sharp contrast to a downtown filled with stately, half-burned buildings with saplings growing from rooftops and terraces. A fire took much of the area in a single night in 1997: what survived still stands. Boarded-up stores are emblazoned with fancy, loping mid-century fonts; there are signs for chains that haven't existed for decades. It's strange, impossible, and beautiful, the Pompeii of the Midwest, a rotting monument to industrialization, an apocalypse fueled by plant-closings, white flight and arson.

The Jacksons left Gary in 1968, right before the Steel City began its freefall: Between 1960 and 2000, the city's population was nearly halved. Their house shows no mark of its former occupants' success, save for the renamed streets—it sits at the corner of Jackson Street and Jackson Family Boulevard. It's incredible to imagine that a family of 11 once lived in the tiny two-bedroom bungalow. There is no garage. Maybe there was, once. Maybe they just practiced in the yard, though dancing in the grass is hard. Maybe there's a basement we don't know about.

When we roll up to 2300 Jackson, it's almost 11 p.m., maybe seven hours since the news hit. Slow-cruising cars blare different eras of MJ as two thick cops parked on ATVs shine their headlights on the crowd milling in the yard. This is not so much a gathering as a looky-loo, a chance to observe the coterie of stuffed animals and notebook-paper tributes. A Gary Fire Department shirt on a hanger clings to the front window's security bars with a note taped to it: "Goodbye Michael J5 forever." There's not a lot of talking up by the actual shrine and its safety candles: Everyone just snaps pictures with their cell phones and slaps at mosquitoes. Some people are crying.

Back at the edge of the yard, locals trade stories, theories and first-hand reminiscences: Michael's appearance at a Gary high school in 2003, older siblings who went to high school with Tito, guesses of what will become of the house. Everyone weighs in on where he'll be buried: Everyone hopes for Gary, thinks it should be Gary— maybe even right here in the backyard. I imagine the tiny, fenced-in lot overtaken by a mausoleum, ringed with teddy bears and white gloves.

The next day, Mayor Rudy Clay talks of turning the house, which would take four minutes (max) to thoroughly examine, into a Graceland. Grim as it is, Jackson's death could mean new life for Gary. A stretch of downtown is set to be razed in the next year: No doubt an MJ shrine will be its star attraction. Interviewing residents a few years back, the idea that Michael could return and somehow save their seemingly unsaveable city was a collectively-held notion. Some held his abandonment against him and considered such a return his duty as a native son, while others were sympathetic—why would the King of Pop ever want to come back to Gary? Few had guessed that this is how it might happen.

The mosquitoes are getting to us, and we've taken all the pictures we can of the memorial heap of mini-mart roses and stuffed animals. Across the street, a man affixes a flashlight to a lawnmower, fires it up, and starts cutting the grass. We get back in the car. On our way out, we stop and take pictures of the long-abandoned Palace Theatre's marquee. Since Donald Trump had the place spruced up for the 2002 Miss USA pageant, it has read "Jackson Five Tonite"—another fantasy future for the Magic City, come and gone.

SUPERCHUNK: I HATE MUSIC

SPIN **magazine, August 2013**

Death is everywhere on *I Hate Music,* Superchunk's 10th studio album. Sidling right beside us, doing air-guitar windmills on
his scythe, from album opener "Overflows" (where "dead" is the
third word frontman Mac McCaughan sings) all the way to bitter-
sweet-ever-after closer "What Can We Do." This is a record of grief,
bristling with the anguish of what it means to survive, to re-evaluate
your life after someone else's death: "Everything is different / Everything is the same."

As if that wasn't quite brutal enough, McCaughan also dredges
up a rhetorical question from that emotional swampland of punk-
after-35: *What does music mean in the face of mortality?* "I hate
music / What is it worth?" goes the opening salvo to "Me & You &
Jackie Mittoo." "Can't bring anyone back to this earth." It's a line
that pulls you up short—after decades of insisting this song or that
album "saved your life," you're suddenly confronted with the fact
that *it actually won't*. It can't.

It's a line that leaves you embarrassed in your vulnerability; to have
ever asserted otherwise seems like a denial of life's terms. When
you are past that youthful period when your whole identity is tied
up in a faith affirmed by music, when the mortal aspects of life start
to catch up with you—*how do you orient yourself?* The small god
who lives in a perfect beat or solo, in the raw, chest-beating howl of
some puerile punk... Is that the same god we curse out and bargain
with when we are trying to keep the people we love here with us?
On this album, McCaughan reckons with this belief system that has
informed so much of his life. Yet the idea that *music is everything*
is rather naive on this side of 40, and saying *music is nothing* is too
hopeless, too cynical, it disorients the past. What to cling to?

I Hate Music is crushing in its poignancy, its ruthless weighing of
what this whole mess adds up to (or doesn't). "Put up your feet on
the dash," McCaughan cheers; he's doing the math on life's beauty
to agony ratio, reasoning with memories from before his friend's
death and after. *I Hate Music* acknowledges music's power to bless
us with meaningful distraction. It can distract us from our mourn-

ing, too, though that's all it can do; grief and music both have the power to distort reality as much as they cut through the bullshit of it all. Title aside, *I Hate Music* eventually (thankfully) comes down on the "everything" side of the argument.

All this is a heavier orbit than the usual "Teenage angst has paid off well / Now I'm bored and old" sentiment of post-punk forty-somethings singing of their disenfranchisement from the scene they built. Chalk it up to the liberation of middle age or the certainty of an audience that has held fast (and aged with them), but the band clearly feels no compulsion to keep it light; they trust their music to hold up under all the heaviness of such examinations and trust us to be able to handle it as well.

All the frustration and anger at play on *I Hate Music* energizes songs like "Staying Home," wherein the Hüsker Dü echoes that have trailed McCaughan since 1991's "Cast Iron" have never been louder (the last thing you expect 10 albums in are Superchunk breaknecking like it's *Land Speed Record* or bust). Ironically, it's an anthem about *not* going out—the ultimate geezer cop-out—set to hardcore, the very sound of youthful vigor. Out of step, indeed. Other songs sit in awe of death, alive in the fresh hell of it, McCaughan's eager-teen squeak of a voice still stretching toward those high notes. His voice is full of love and restless sadness, which tells as much of a story as the lyrics do, atop heartbreaking lines like "Oh, what I'd do / To waste an afternoon with you."

It's a perfect place for Superchunk to wind up, given this is a band that initially wooed us 25 years ago with "Slack Motherfucker," indie rock's quintessential bratty-kid anthem. Now, just as confidently, they have given us songs that map adult life, even if these anthems are more a mortality blues. But with *I Hate Music*, Superchunk prove that it wasn't naive to believe in what music could do.

BETWEEN THE VIADUCT OF YOUR DREAMS: ON VAN MORRISON

TINYLUCKYGENIUS, July 2008

When the chasm of human experience feels unbridgeable, and the past is keeping you like the stocks, and there is no absolution to be had, no forgiveness to salve you, and the world feels too much in its infinite newness and it's midnight and people are screaming and feeding babies ranch-flavor chicken fingers from a bucket, when all you see is difference and a long string of your own unqualified failures, there is Van singing, "Lay me down...to be born again." There is so much wanting in "Astral Weeks," but it's not desperation, it's all vessel; it's faith enough to cover us all. He waits until 4:55 to slip the big one, "I'm nothin but a stranger in this world"—after he's sung all this future-hope, he's just fucking untangled joy over pipping flutes—here, he flashes his wretch-like-me makings, and dovetails his abyss with deliverance—there is something beyond this—he sounds like he's about to giggle he's so delighted, he's so *sure*. It's fine, fixed sureness, an easy sureness when he repeats it this last time, in this final, ecclesiastic glee coda. He has all the reasons not to believe, but he does. The Buddhists say hope is a trap, it's a set up for suffering, but the hope in this song, it is free, it drags nothing with, it is only onward, onward in love and frailty.

PART SIX

BAD REVIEWS

MILEY CYRUS / *BANGERZ*

***SPIN* magazine, October 2013**

What is there to "review" when it comes to a Miley Cyrus album? Her singing, affected and perfected by software? How her powerless pop makes you feel, deep down in your quivering soul? How to rate this latest iteration of her personae—code name: "strategic hot mess"—to address these complex matters of cultural ownership with a post-teen girl who has belonged to the public her whole life, a simulacrum of girlhood turned into one of the great products of our age, a bigger emblem of the empire than Mickey Mouse himself? What else could she do but nuke it, saturate herself in our greedy gaze until she dissolves, give it all away, turn herself out until our knowledge of her is borderline gynecological? Is there a part of Miley that remains unknown? Did you really expect an album called *Bangerz* to reveal anything to you?

In knowing everything, we find we know nothing. The entertainment value of Cyrus' work is more than simply typical pop pleasure: It is the slow-motion horror of watching toxic sleaze replace toxic purity (cf. Dave Hickey). At her extremes, she firmly engaged our most puritanical mores—from saccharine virgin to knowingly fellating a sledgehammer—Cyrus is, at once, both banal and pernicious.

Though *Bangerz* may seem like some sort of sudden, shocking transgression, grinding gears as Cyrus shifts from Disney World to Worldstar, 2009's "Party in the U.S.A." foretold it all: the wow and much-ness of fame, Jay-Z on the radio. Cyrus has touted this album as "sexy" (ehh), "believable" and "very adult." Though only the latter rings true—in the traditional, male-fantasy-driven, pornographic sense of "adult"—her actions, and even more so her inactions, conform to the arc of most mainstream adult entertainment. Here, she's often pliant and naive, begging to serve, or at least be noticed and deemed worthy. On the Pharell-penned "#GETITRIGHT," she lays in bed, powerless and horny, overcome and waiting to be activated by male desire; on "My Darlin'," she solicits the revivifying attentions of a dude who is just not that into her; on "Maybe You're Right" and "FU," she leaves; and on "SMS," she alludes to taking her satisfaction into her own hands, but it's all played for (what else?) titillation.

On the other three tracks, she's don't-give-a-fuck, she's crazy, she's partying, she's doing her bitch-bad thing. It's all very familiar-sounding-and-feeling, and it should be: "Wrecking Ball" gives co-writing credit to Sasha Karbeck, who helped pen "Born to Die" and "Paradise" for Lana Del Rey; also credited are Dr. Luke and Cirkut, the team behind (most recently) Katy Perry's "Roar." *Bangerz* is a precise album that flits between bombastic and turgid; it is not very fun.

It's strange to think that anyone could find this record offensive or controversial. What are we even to extract from *Bangerz* about the interior life of someone who reported her true liberation was driving an Explorer down Philly's South Street, a cheap chain standing in for her zipless fuck—a glance into a fantasy life unlived? Is her woman-spurned exultation as powerful as the version Katy Perry sells to us? Is her pathos as grand as Rihanna's? Her pleasure as real?

Though Cyrus has a lovely, albeit generic voice, singing is not her truest gift; instead, it's the sheer quality of her mirroring, the way she gives us exactly what we want in lethal doses, grinding against our most American horror. As Pharrell himself says in the new MTV doc *Miley Cyrus: The Movement*, "Why is she doing this? Because she's a product of America." She's playing it like a rebel, but she's simply being who we've goaded her to be.

NU AGE: ANIMAL COLLECTIVE AND BELL ORCHESTRE

Chicago Reader, **November 2005**

To invoke the Minutemen: *Do you want new wave or do you want the truth?* Here we are, 20 years later, and the new wave sounds more and more like old New Age. We're dealing with a fresh crop of musicians who pass off extreme indulgence as experimentalism and neck beards as a sign of higher consciousness. They cite barely Googleable influences so we won't notice the similarities between them and, say, any popular jam band or latter-day solo album by a member of Tangerine Dream. There are a bunch of names floating around for this stuff—nu-folk, freak-folk, New Weird America—but I have my own: new-jack hippy-wave (when I am feeling gracious) or downtown bullshit city (the rest of the time). Why, you may ask, am I hating on both the player and the game? Simple: I do not like being lied to. And the truth is there is no new in this new.

Bell Orchestre, the all-instrumental chamber orchestra side project of Arcade Fire members Richard Reed Parry and Sarah Neufeld, might sell a gazillion copies of their debut, *Recording a Tape the Color of Light* (Rough Trade), based on association alone. It's the sort of thing that might appeal to anyone looking for a more "sophisticated" variation on the irresistible pop drama we've come to expect from their other band. Though I hate to dash the hopes a 7.9 rating from *Pitchfork* instills, unless some consensual, messy frottage between Mike Oldfield and Jean-Luc Ponty is what you're scouring the bins for, consider your parade urinated upon.

The bio that came with the BO record cites the Penguin Cafe Orchestra, the Kronos Quartet, and Arvo Part as influences, which is not only wishful thinking but perhaps a touch perverted, even by the standards of publicist-spun hyperbole. Bell Orchestre has all the ingredients for classical gas—French horn, upright bass, violin and trumpet—but none of the dexterity or seriousness. They're content with pomp and cheeze, the sort of ham-fisted slop best suited to close-ups of a windswept Leonardo DiCaprio on the deck of the Titanic or a 2006 off-road vehicle taking the corners of a majestic mountainside in a commercial. Sure: if you're 19 and "House of Jealous Lovers" is your "Houses of the Holy," then some dog-food-grade violin compositions kicked "disco" with brass and a 4/4 hi-hat beat might sound light years ahead as they pop out of your computer speakers. But let's not sully the work of a 70-year-old Estonian composer known for his subtle dissonance by connecting it to some Suzuki-method yo-yos from Montreal.

Don't get me wrong: Bell Orchestre has dynamics. Strings purr against some really funky chimes, then build, get quiet—and build again! And there's unsubtle discord in the horn arrangements: the trumpet-French horn duel that drops like a wet turd from the sky a minute and four seconds into "Les Lumieres Pt. 2" sounds like a death match between first chairs in a high school band. It'll make you wish they'd quit the song after Pt. 1. Recording melds the push-button dynamics and overwrought gesticulation of a *Billboard*-charting emo band with the edginess of a Windham Hill sampler, and if you're thinking it doesn't get much worse than that, rest assured: you are correct.

Meanwhile, somewhere in Brooklyn sits poor Animal Collective, a group whose best intentions have clearly curdled. Avey Tare, Panda Bear, Geologist and Deakin issued four albums before their breakthrough 2004 release *Sung Tongs*. Their fresh dispatch, *Feels* (Fat Cat), is a muddled mess, and does the freak-folk ho show with which the band is associated no favors. Perhaps Geologist and Deakin—who didn't participate on *Sung Tongs* but are now back in the mix—are to blame.

Feels fails in all the ways that *Sung Tongs* worked: Where their layered sound-on-sound psych-out was once deep and expansive, now it's sloppy and impenetrable. These are hookless songs buried under a landslide of trebly collage. And with seven of the nine tracks running in excess of five minutes, it's apparent that AC lacks not only any clue of how to build songs, but also the ability to control them.

Boring is one thing; trying to pass off massage music as experimental is another. *Feels* is the sort of album meant to be augmented by the sound of a $39 feng shui fountain percolating in the background, because nothing goes with a gurgling plug-in waterspout like songs with copious amounts of zither.

The only things keeping Animal Collective from losing their way in the mist are a couple of up-tempo tracks—"Did You See the Words" and "The Purple Bottle"—and the lyrics, which had me recalling (not so fondly) the first time I took acid, in ninth grade, and spent two hours dealing with a talking enchilada entrée. One minute they're singing about staring into a mirror naked and the next they're screaming about a hot tub: it's like some Bret Easton Ellis nightmare starring Jim Morrison. Also, a note to whichever member is responsible for the eleventy-hundred tracks of piano on this album: dude, it's cool to lay off the sustain pedal sometimes, nothing bad will happen. Especially when you're already dealing with endless tracks of tape delay, loops of percolating bong hits, men imitating roosters, real birds chirping, dulcimer, pennywhistle, and a quartet of aesthetes channeling their spirit animals while a bell chimes in the distance.

Don't be fooled into thinking Animal Collective's recent collaboration with neofolk icon Vashti Bunyan is a sign of their psych authority—if *Feels* is to be taken at face value, they'll be foisting Andreas Vollenweider on us next.

TYLER, THE CREATOR: *WOLF*
SPIN magazine, April 2005

It's easy to understand why the Internet swooned so hard when Tyler, The Creator first floated along and pricked our bubble. In 2010, hip-hop was mostly a bunch of old, rich dudes resting hard on their old, rich-dude laurels; Odd Future were all manner of teenage lewdness, Fuck You heroes, too much talent and no dough. They were the punkest thing to happen to hip-hop since Jesus was a boy. At their molten center, Tyler emerged as a roach-swallowing *emcee terrible*, a seething-in-self-loathing, Eminem-weaned skate rat doling harsh tokes just for the delight of seeing olds squirm. He wasn't interested in being hip-hop's messiah as much as its smirking antichrist.

Last year, in these very pages, Tyler prepped us for the evolution we should expect on *Wolf*—now that he's found success, he's gotta rap about what he's reaping; it would be disingenuous to front like he's still sleeping on a couch. A quick inventory of what *Goblin*-success wrought: a four-story house, European model pussy, QT with Bieber. He fessed that he'd grown weary of that imma-rape-you steez, so there's none of that here (it's cool brah, Rick Ross got you covered). Tyler's created tangible distance from the bratty rage of, say, *Bastard*'s "AssMilk,"—the girls on *Wolf* are all alive and willing.

The album loosely follows a discursive story involving Tyler's alter-ego, Wolf, and his id, Sam, and a shared love interest, Salem. The story occupies maybe half the album—it's sometimes hard to parse the characters, aside from that Sam is a bit of a *Bastard* throw-back, with his murderous bent and punctuating lines with "faggot." The stories sparking point, "Awkward," is one of *Wolf*'s highlights. An epigrammatic love story born of a mall date, Tyler's voice pitch-shifted down to his Wolf-growl, he gets goofy on a girl whose eyes are the color of weed and makes entreaties for hand holding over analog synth ambience. "You're my girl, whether you like it or not," he pouts. *Wolf, what have you done with our beloved brat, Tyler?*

He soon reappears, unfortunately. As good as "Awkward" is, like much of the album, it feels like an audition; Tyler flaunts his range as a producer and MC, clearly vying to transcend the shock-and-awe rep that has preceded him. But for much of the rest of *Wolf*'s woefully uneven, wildly indulgent, 18-track slog, that rep drags him, and us, back down. All that is alive and compelling here (say, the RAMP-smooth soul-jazz posse cut "Rusty") begins to dissolve as we pass the 60-minute mark. While a duet between Stereolab's Laetitia Sadier and Frank Ocean sounds promising on paper, it comes at the end of the nearly eight-minute song suite "PartyIsntOver/Campfire/Bimmer," which, by the time you've reached the Bieber-rejected closing third, feels like it's about 16 BPM and slowing.

There is some dexterity within *Wolf*'s production—the antic "Tamale," is the kind of M.I.A. song M.I.A. doesn't make anymore, "Trashwang," is a skittering, trap-parody posse cut featuring Trash Talk that approximates the anarchy of vintage Odd Future. But cuts like "48" sound like a tribute to diminishing-returns era N*E*R*D. It's a weird look for a kid that is supposedly hip-hop's vanguard, to be so caught up in work that sounds like it's sole purpose is to impress Pharrell by approximating his style. The album crests early with "Awkward," the single "Domo23," and "Answer," which all run back to back, and then runs another eight songs until we can discern a pulse again on the Earl verse of "Rusty."

While it's inarguable that Tyler's become more sophisticated as a producer, he's clearly trying to prove and disprove our understanding of his image, and at a loss for how to orient himself now that he's cosseted by a rabid fanbase and an awed, fearful industry that he's spent the last few years flipping off. Tyler's whole story was how this skate-rat outsider made the *Billboard* Top 10 on a record he made in a garage with his friends. Now he's ceded all of that to become the ultimate insider—making studio albums with marquee names (Pharrell, Erykah, his Grammy-nommed homie Frank Ocean), boasting of his money and copious tour strange, whining about the burdens of fame. "Colossus," for example, uncharitably bristles at his Stans, who sound like regular, engaged, reasonable fans, but are nonetheless dismissed here as posers and, yes, "fags."

Which brings us to *Wolf*'s most grievous misstep, and its one true spiritual connection to the superior *Bastard* and *Goblin*: Tyler's defiant use of the word "faggot." As usual, he spends a ton of time here bragging about how little he cares about how the world sees him, but his reliance on the other f-bomb to keep our attention suggests otherwise. In a recent *LA Weekly* interview, he dismissed concern about the slur: "I wasn't using 'fag' to refer to gay people. If I call a piece of lettuce a faggot, am I homophobic? I might be anti-lettuce, but...." Now, on "Domo23," he brushes off the almost-protest that marred his appearance at last year's Pitchfork Festival, holding up his proximity to queerness (scoffing at those critics "claiming I hate gays even though Frank is on 10 of my songs") as proof he's not a homophobe.

He may not be—and that's the rub. Tyler's trying to have it both ways: going for cheap shots and playing ignorant, as if a straight boy can recontextualize a slur that has been used to humiliate and dehumanize gay people for decades, despite using the word *just like the people who mean it* do. On *Wolf,* he banks on the word's awful power to show us what a bad boy he still is, which is tantamount to saying "faggot" and actually meaning it. We showed Tyler where it hurts and so that's where he sticks the knife. He degrades the value of his own art for the sake of seeming raw, the same old unfiltered Tyler.

That Tyler brand identity depends on outrage and rejection by scandalized adults. Odd Future has always been about exclusion, about making sure that there is a dividing line between Them and Us, and if you don't get it, the joke is on you. But in an era where the queering of hip-hop is the genre's biggest story (ironically, one that Odd Future's out members Syd the Kid and Frank Ocean helped foment), Tyler's insistence on using "fag" just to show how transgressive he is leaves him in the dust, as the real punks (Le1f, Angel Haze, Mykki Blanco, Frank, et al.) truly advance the game. Tyler's increasing fame has made him unremarkable; his desperation to be shocking has reduced him a joke.

OLD YEAR'S END

TINYLUCKYGENIUS, December 2007

No year-end lists to contribute to for any publication this year. Budget constraints, art constraints, being freelance are most of the reasons. It's perfectly fine, because "best" is disturbingly open-ended, and what difference does a year make when art is currently only truly divisible into pre- or post-9/11, pre- or post-Katrina, and—save for that effluvient noise coming from down the hall—it's all popular music, and there is less meaning and more money than ever in anything you might be tempted to call underground. More people getting more rich on a myth is a terribly old story I'm not much interested in anyhow. It's also perfectly fine because I'm not sure I can name a couple 2007 LPs that I listened to again 'n' again, all the way through, for pleasure, that brought me pleasure, that I felt like I understood, or could campaign behind.

Part of the reason behind that was simply, or maybe sadly(?), constraints of the job. This year, almost all of the money I made writing was in blurbs, charticles and show previews that are between 300 and 80 words instead of essays. I had to write way more stuff, but with not much space to extrapolate on big ideas (if the band even has them) or theories (if I even can conjure them), and what I write is more about the "good vs. bad," interesting vs. not, and then make a joke or two. How I make money necessitated a change in what I listen to and how I listen to it in 2007. I ain't complaining; I'm lucky to squeeze paychecks out of it. In the meanwhile, look for my byline on the inflight mag next time you fly from Duluth to Phoenix.

Nonetheless, I'm not bummed about the non-existence of a year-end list. Hierarchy is bunk. Plus, you already know that the M.I.A. record is serious business, though her live show made me feel like she's a polemicized Dan Deacon for those who are down with *othering* and have the mp3 blog to prove it. I think PJ Harvey making a record from the POV of a Victorian-era ghost baby is really interesting. Best? As best as the zillion Lil Wayne songs that I downloaded this summer? *I have no idea.* Probably not. As best as Mika Miko doing "Attitude"? Defs not as best as how Mama Chancla stunk *after* singing "Attitude." I do not know if Radiohead is best because I haven't downloaded it because I can't decide how much I want to pay for it. Not sure if Radiohead has as much fuck-the-man bestness as the mail order-only edition of 100 cassettes that Rjyan and Roby put out. Or the Landlord demo-cassette that the kid at the farmers' market passed me. Is free, invisible, green, non-corpo action from a band that makes approx. a million dollars a show or free, hand-to-hand, traditional sharing of *the people's medium** (*pre-Internet version) more of a BEST remix of anti-capitalist ideal? You can't really tie best. Another best is the differential between No Age on record and No Age on the stage which revealed that America's favorite Angeleno cool dude dual/duel/duo is *making punk a threat again.* I am not sure how it's "best" compared with when I went to see Watain and their corpse paint had so much realistic peeling skin that it made me gag a little and leave after a few songs because they were an actually-scary black metal band. Though were their costumes as best as the kid at Fiery Furnaces' Halloween show dressed as a furnace on fire? What is best between scariest and charming effort? Watching Tim Kinsella turn over a new solo leaf, as a singer-singer songwriter, baring all and inspiring a very mortal tremble amongst the 22 or 34 people watching on a Free Monday at the Bottle, his married/buried allegories the most powerful take since "All Apologies"; I had to leave because it was so good. I couldn't take it. Another song more and there'd be some unmooring of internal paradigm. There was also that backyard party Bird Names show which was a wretched best—I felt my age ruefully and deeply and then during the show, suddenly, an epoch lifted amongst the sweat and flashing xmas lights.

Yeasayer might of made the best of the TV on the Radio rip-off albums of 2007, but that dude's got a fretless bass, so I might have to defer to Dragons of Zynth, who have one great song that out-TV-on-the-Radio's TV on the Radio. Like most people, I also like the bands that sound like my favorite band. Generally, the last thing I want to admit—that I'll settle for a cheap imitation. As a best, it was not as best as Rickie Lee Jones singing about the garden of Gethsemane, or the Michael Dracula album. Michael Dracula is a girl who sings like she is very high, cold and careful. Static doom and a certain intransigence is why I think people like, say, Wooden Shjips, but 10-minute songs are a lot to ask of people, and I'm still not feeling hippydroneshit as the new punxsound, so I go for Michael Dracula. I also thought that Lavender Diamond was going to be best, but I keep forgetting to listen to it a third time. Those first two? Wonderful. It'll make you feel like a virgin again.

NEVERMIND ALREADY:
NIRVANA'S 20TH ANNIVERSARY BOXSET
Chicago Reader, **September 2011**

Kurt Cobain died for somebody's sins, but not mine. The anointed grunge Buddha is as big now as he's ever been, which is to say nearly ubiquitous. When *Nevermind* hit number one, less than four months after its release, it was selling roughly 1.2 million copies a month. No one sells like that anymore and no one ever will again, but Nirvana is still popular—and Cobain even more so. Within the past five years he's knocked Elvis out of the number one spot on *Forbes'* list of top-earning dead celebrities; you can own him as a figurine or on a lunch box, or you can buy pre-ratty, Cobain-edition Converse and cultivate your own aura of junkie manqué.

It's hard to believe that 20 years have gone by since *Nevermind* came along and changed everything. And it's hard to imagine an album doing that now, even if we had a fully-functioning record industry. Nirvana's supersize ghost lingers in our hearts, and every few years the corpo-coffers get to clangin' hungrily for every last penny in the pockets of anyone that's ever had a head-shop Cobain poster pinned to their bedroom wall.

Nirvana retrospectives and reissues to date include the live *From the Muddy Banks of the Wishkah* (1996), a no-nonsense best-of simply called *Nirvana* (2002), the weighty, rarities set *With the Lights Out* (2004), a best-of culled from that set called *Sliver: The Best of the Box* (2005), *Live at Reading* (2009), and vinyl reissues over the past two years of *Bleach, Nevermind, In Utero* and *Unplugged*. Now, with '90s grunge nostalgia at high tide, Universal is releasing one of the bone-driest offerings yet. The "super deluxe" four-CD/one-DVD 20th-anniversary version of *Nevermind*, which comes out on Tuesday, is built around two different mixes of the album—as if anyone listening on earbuds on a city bus is going to be able to tell them apart, or cares to A/B them. Does anyone imagine that kids deafened by two decades of increasingly shitty mastering and overcompression will even be able to even hear the difference between the familiar Andy Wallace radio polish (most of disc one) and the initial Butch Vig mix (all of disc three), which still has some punk blood coursing through its bass rumble?

The Vig mix made the rounds as a bootleg not long after *Nevermind* hit big, as did the April 1990, pre-Grohl demos recorded at Smart Studios (part of disc two), and reveal nothing except that Chad Channing was the inferior drummer. There are eight boom-box tracks from the band's rehearsal space (most of the rest of disc two), but their novelty is short-lived. Who wants to listen to any band's scuzzed-up cassette -tape demos? Every track that wasn't on the original release of *Nevermind*—the BBC sessions, the B sides—has already been well circulated as a bootleg or seen proper release in a better form. And what's on disc four and the accompanying DVD? The reliable filler of live recordings. *Zzzzz* and good night.

Nevermind is a great record, but lord, what a boring thing to offer fans. There's not even any fresh meat for the obsessives who go for this sort of thing. Yet this bottom-of-the-barrel commemoration also carries wonderful news: there's nothing left to scrape up. The lost tracks, alternate versions, outtakes, live sets, piss takes and demos have all been packaged and turned out. His former labels have had 17 years to weave those scraps into dollars—and they're clearly diluting what few bits are left in order to make it last. Universal is stacking up the editions of *Nevermind* for a last hurrah, with not just the "super deluxe" set but also a two-disc "deluxe" version and a straight-up single-CD remastered reissue of the album. Oh, and you can buy the DVD by itself, too. This is the beginning of the end—though if you squint, you can see the "Heart-Shaped Box in an Actual Box Shaped Like a Heart 25th Anniversary Boxset" and "Nevermind in Mono" galloping this way on the horizon.

It's funny, this latest *Nevermind* coming down the pike two weeks after *Winterland*, a five-CD/nine-LP box of live Jimi Hendrix recordings from 1968. Hendrix is, of course, the most repackaged and reissued artist we've got—a model provider for the dying major labels. Hardly a holiday shopping season has passed in recent memory when he wasn't revivified in some slick, immodest box. Nirvana, as this pitiful set makes clear, doesn't have such an infinitely expandable catalog. Cobain is not our Jimi—he's our Jim. Nirvana, punk bona fides be damned, has become an analogue to The Doors for today's misunderstood, stoned teenagers: a died-young druggie poet-totem.

Cobain's nasty, sudden exit at the height of his fame ensures we will always wish for more. These endless reissues count on that. These boxes and anniversary editions prey upon the universal, inchoate wish to relive the singular moment of "Smells Like Teen Spirit." That feeling of being possessed by its pure abandon, its stuttering pound, the implacable tension between verse and chorus, the feral grain of Cobain's voice. There is not a one among us that cannot pinpoint where we were and what we were doing, what we felt hearing it for the first time. That wish is there in anyone who ever heard Nirvana and loved them. But you never get as high as the first time.

This is clearly understood by every company that owns a piece (labels, publishing houses), everyone with a claim to stake (Love, Grohl, Novoselic), and everybody with some marketable crumb to pimp out (Michael Azerrad, for instance, has made plenty of hay with his Cobain interview tapes). And Cobain, whose heart once beat heavy with Olympia-bred punk dogma, isn't here to refuse any of it. *He's dead—so fuck him.* In life he was a commodity, in death, even more so. As Everett True wrote in 2007's *Nirvana: The Biography*, the intervention staged shortly before Cobain's suicide focused as much on getting him into rehab as it did on cajoling him into headlining Lollapalooza. Now he's no longer an impediment to anyone's potential revenue stream.

It's easy to speculate about what Cobain and Nirvana would have become had he lived. The band's next album could've been a *Chinese Democracy*-like fiasco, especially embarrassing in light of Cobain's original genius-flash. He could've gone Corgan and released music with steadily diminishing returns for a decade plus. He could've joined the Foo Fighters. He could've taken the Reznor path, "retiring" after a steady, respectable career. (Who knew then that Eddie Vedder would turn out to be the real punk among Cobain's grunge-era "peers?") Revisiting *Nevermind* is like flexing a phantom limb made up of Nirvana records that never were. That's all it means now, all that's left—fantasy. The tomb is empty; let the dead buy the dead.

PART
SEVEN

STRICTLY
BUSINESS

PUNK IS DEAD! LONG LIVE PUNK!: A REPORT ON THE STATE OF TEEN SPIRIT FROM THE MOBILE SHOPPING MALL THAT IS THE VANS WARPED TOUR

Chicago Reader, **August 2004**

Teenagers are the most powerful audience in America, and this summer the Vans Warped Tour—which began June 25 in Houston and ends today, August 20, in Boston—celebrated ten years of unwavering devotion to this principle. At each stop anywhere from 10,000 to 30,000 teenagers converged on a parking lot, a stadium, or an amphitheater, wading deep into the froth of pop-cultural commerce that they drive with their fickle tastes. In exchange for the $18 to $30 that a Warped ticket cost, the sunburned throngs got eight hours and five dozen bands of accessible punk, hardcore and hip-hop.

Yet, no impartial observer could conclude that Warped is first and foremost about the music. It's about teenagers and their disposable income. Punk in its primal form is, of course, an anti-commercial genre, but Warped has turned money into the medium of cultural affiliation here, as it already was everywhere else. What's being sold is an entrée into punk, and most of the fans are too new to the music's ideals to understand that they're buying a version of fuck-all rebellion that's been repackaged by businesspeople. Or maybe they do understand, and they come because they think it's the only version left. Warped is a mammoth shopping and marketing experience, a towering conglomerated product of the Clear Channel Age, and though the music is the initial draw, purchases are the way the kids express themselves to themselves, to the bands, and to each other.

Look no further than The Casualties' merch tent, with its 24 T-shirt designs, two styles of handkerchief, and three different hats. A day at Warped is about kids saying "I love you" to their favorite bands, with cash in hand, on a scale that boggles the mind. We're a long way from the Fireside Bowl, which is the kind of punk dive many Warped acts came up playing, sometimes to only 20 or 30 kids at a time. Selling a handful of seven-inches for gas money isn't gonna cut it if you're touring as part of an operation that requires a fleet of ten tractor-trailers, a hundred tour buses and vans, 11 sound systems, a full-time on-site doctor and massage therapist, and a catering service that can handle two hot meals a day for 650 to 800 people. On July 24, the day Warped stopped at the Tweeter Center in Tinley Park, the band Taking Back Sunday grossed $20,000 in T-shirt sales alone.

I spent a few weeks on the 2004 Warped Tour among these teenagers—the average age seemed to be 16. I remember 16 as a pretty grim year, but from the safe distance of a decade, 16-year-olds are completely fascinating. I was surrounded by thousands of kids, a rushing tide of adolescent self-concept run riot, of bad tribal tattoos and rapturous infatuations and questionable hairstyles, all reeking of the pungent desire to simultaneously transgress and fit in perfectly.

This unselfconscious incoherence is a magnificent thing to behold. These kids all seemed to have a flawless idea of who they were—or who they wanted to seem to be, with their carefully arranged ensembles of brand names, slogans and symbols—and absolutely no idea how they actually appeared. I saw boys milling around a San Diego sports pavilion parking lot, chewing on corn dogs and wearing mesh-back caps reading "My Balls Itch" at 11 a.m. on a Sunday. I saw a girl with the name of every act on the tour written in pen down the legs of her jeans—apparently signifying an impulse to identify with simply being at a "punk concert" more than loyalty to any of the actual bands. None of this, of course, was any less honest for being so obviously calculated—even when you're a teenager faking it, approximating a borrowed notion of cool, you're still bound to be more real, more transparent and more vulnerable than any adult.

The second thing you notice at Warped is the din. At any given moment there were at least four bands playing on the sprawling carnival midway of the concert campus. Most festivals make do with a single main stage and one or two distraction stages, but Warped was operating four main stages, four secondary stages and a handful of stages-in-name-only—usually just a canopy in front of a van or a strip of grass between a set of PA speakers. The Brian Stage and the Teal Stage were for the headliners—and when a band on Brian finished its set, another band cranked up on Teal within three minutes. You could watch NOFX, Alkaline Trio, The Sounds and Yellowcard back-to-back simply by ping-ponging 100 feet to the left or right. Next year's headliners apparent (Rufio, My Chemical Romance, The Casualties) played on the Maurice Stage and the Volcom-sponsored stage, also side by side. Shunted out into the general population, next to the merch booths, were smaller elevated stages sponsored by Smartpunk, Punkrocks.net and Ernie Ball. The Hurley/Kevin Says Stage, barely a stage at all, was a slab of linoleum flooring with yellow caution tape strung along the front.

With so many bands playing at once, not even the most dedicated fan could see everything. Like a shopping mall, the concert campus was designed to keep customers circulating, to induce them to check out every tent and booth at least once. Warped has even developed an ingenious strategy to bring the kids in early and keep them all day—the lineup of set times was different at every stop, and wasn't announced in advance. Though technically a headliner, Bad Religion might have been playing at noon rather than taking the day's last slot at 7:30 p.m. Thursday might have been slated for 1 p.m. or 5:15 p.m., and you couldn't know till you got past the gate. So you'd show up at 11 in the morning and find out that your two favorite bands were going on at noon and 6 p.m. What to do with the hours in-between? There were band booths and label booths. There were good-cause booths: PETA, breast cancer awareness, Take Action! (progressive activism and "personal empowerment"). And then there were booths for the likes of Slim Jims (free wristbands and meat sticks!), Cingular Wireless (plastic gems and band stickers to decorate your cell phone!), and Dodge (custom racing cars in a showroom tent!). You could get your merch, purse or person autographed, sign up for 100 different mailing lists, try out a bass, get your hair shaved into a Mohawk for free, or chew some complimentary Wrigley's Winterfresh gum. You could also buy stuff: sneakers, a skateboard deck, a hot dog, a hemp necklace, lemonade, band stickers or pins, spiked leather wristbands, thong underwear, a furry neon belt, sunglasses, a pizza from Domino's, a shirt that said "I'm sick and tired of white girls."

The hip-hop tent, dubbed the Code of the Cutz Stage, offered the only respite from the ever-present feeling of being marketed to. The dozen or so acts in the rotating daily lineup often left the stage, rubbing elbows with the crowd, or ventured outside the tent, mic in hand—I saw Connecticut rapper ADM (from the duo Glue) holding forth from atop the nearby picnic tables. It's not like there was no selling going on here, but it wasn't the faceless, focus-grouped variety: the Code of the Cutz performers frequently hawked their own CDs and shirts outside the tent after their sets. They were also pushing some of the most aggressive political agendas on the tour. NOFX, masterminds of Rock Against Bush, may pause between songs to wish Dick Cheney a heart attack, and Yellowcard may beg kids to get off their asses and vote, but those gestures seem rote next to Non Phixion freestyling on the human impact of unfair drug-sentencing laws or Immortal Technique calling Condi Rice "the new age Sally Hemings."

On July 20 in Milwaukee, I hung out with a friend who ran the Alternative Press autograph booth while he got ready for a Taking Back Sunday signing. (The band's sets were always so mobbed that I never managed to see them from less than a few hundred yards away.) My friend set up stools, laid out fresh Sharpies, stacked posters into huge piles, and shooed too-eager fans back into the quarter-mile line. In front was a boy in a homemade Taking Back Sunday T-shirt: with colored markers he'd written the date, the band's name, some lyrics, and the name of the venue in capital letters, and along the bottom edge in alternating colors was a repeated rickrack ribbon of "Taking Back Sunday * Vans Warped Tour * Taking Back Sunday * Vans Warped Tour." The homemade Warped Commemorative Shirt, Pants, or Hat was common enough to be a phenomenon on the tour. That public display of affection, that preemptive sentimentality pivoting on this exact moment, is what emo has instilled in the culture of punk fandom: advance nostalgia for the peak experience.

The audience at Warped, unlike the sausage party you get at a typical ground-level punk show, is half-female, maybe more. But in San Diego there were only seven women performing, spread across three bands. The Licks drew a screaming, girl-heavy crowd every time they played, though this was their first tour and they didn't even have a CD out yet. Between songs, frontwoman Juliette Lewis fell into a put-on honky-tonk drawl, yelling "This one is for the ladies!" When I saw her, she was wearing a couture T-shirt, a bikini, knee pads, and fingerless gloves, and her makeup was running with sweat. She grabbed her crotch, humped the monitors, threw the horned hand at the crowd, and assumed several different yoga positions. She's lithe and tough, a real performer—judging by how she moves, she's spent much of her life with people staring at her.

In Los Angeles I watched the Mean Reds deliver what would turn out to be the rawest set I'd see on the tour. The Mean Reds are from Tucson and barely a year out of high school. It was only the sixth day of the tour, and they were already on "probation" for running their mouths onstage about what a sold-out, capitalist-pig enterprise Warped is, how it isn't really punk, et cetera. Warped founder and figurehead Kevin Lyman in turn advised the boys to do their homework before letting fly with the rhetoric: Did they think for a minute that he'd invited all those sponsors along for the ride for any other reason than to defray the tour's enormous expenses and keep ticket prices sane? (You might assume a band would give these questions some thought before committing to a couple months on the tour.)

The Mean Reds are oblivious and obnoxious and out of control. They have all the fire of Nation of Ulysses, but instead of suits and manifestos, they have other people's Klonopin prescriptions and women's thrift-store blouses à la Bob Stinson. They look like scumbags who sleep in the desert. I'm not sure they have any idea what they're doing or how great it is. Halfway through their apocalyptic 25-minute set, I told the guy who runs their label that Anthony Anzalone, the singer, reminded me of Darby Crash. The label guy said, "He has no idea who Darby Crash is." He also told me that the band had gotten into music by listening to Nirvana—and that they were recently the subject of a seven-label bidding war but refused all offers.

By the time Warped reached Minneapolis, a little more than three weeks later, the Mean Reds had been kicked off the tour. Their labelmates the Rolling Blackouts had gotten the boot after their singer pissed next to a stage while another band was playing, and Anzalone pissed his pants during a Mean Reds set in solidarity. The Mean Reds are more like the Warped audience than they know—confused, idealistic, angry and furiously trying to slap the world awake and tell it who they think they are.

When I saw the band in L.A., Anzalone was filthy, his sweat making bright stripes in the layer of dirt caked to his skin—he'd made a vow that he wouldn't shower until the band was off the tour, which at the time was still supposed to mean another month and a half. He was shirtless, covered in cuts, and wearing swim trunks, boat shoes, and a wrinkled women's vest with gold anchors on it. He rolled in the grass in front of the stage, right under the yellow caution-tape barrier and into the crowd. The security staff watched with alarm as this yawping kid, pink-faced and exploding, writhed at our feet, humping the grass, grabbing ankles and screaming, "Holla! Playa! Holla! Playa!"

Between songs he contended with the Winterfresh gum camper-van 30 feet away, which was staffed by a chipper woman who leapt into the brief lulls in the Mean Reds' set to announce, via her gum-mobile's large PA, that "Fresh breath and fresh music go together!" Anzalone glanced hatefully at the truck and passed the mic, interviewing the girls in the front row: "What does punk rock mean to you? What is punk rock about for you?"

A Latina no older than 15 with red-streaked hair and matching red bands on her braces answered, "Punk rock is about being who you are and doing what you want." The rest of the small audience clapped.

CHIEF KEEF

Chicago Tribune, **August 2013**

Chief Keef does not want to talk to the *Tribune*. It's been rumored that the first piece of advice Kanye West gave the 17-year-old rapper was to stop doing interviews, and he has seemingly heeded Ye's word. Nonetheless, his management team pleads and cajoles. "The *Tribune* is bigger than the *Red Eye*," says Peeda Pan, one of a fleet of managers who tends to Keef. "It's 12 or 13 times bigger." Keef crosses his arms and purses his lips. "It's for the cover," explains Peeda Pan, punting. "Jay-Z has done the cover. Kanye's done it." With these references to namebrand rappers, it's hard to discern whether they're being dropped because that's who Keef is modeling his career after, or because he believes he merits similar star treatment. The young rapper shakes his head, almost imperceptibly, "no." He is a petulant teen with a superstar's largesse.

It is 6 p.m. on Sunday, the final day of the sold-out Pitchfork Festival and AraabMuzik is onstage making 18,000 people dance. Keef and his crew of 16 (approximately three managers, his publicist, recently-signed rapper Lil Reese, his sometimes-producer 18-year-old Young Chop, a bevy of friends) have just arrived. Keef and Reese are scheduled to make an unannounced two-song cameo appearance during AraabMuzik's set; this will be the biggest hometown audience they've ever played to. As is the custom in hip-hop, Keef and Reese's handlers have demanded payment in full before the two MCs grace the stage. This is not how things usually work at Pitchfork. Pitchfork founder Ryan Schreiber is pacing in tight circles, drawing hard on his cigarette and impatiently redialing his iPhone. The person with the money and the contracts is not picking up. For these two songs, Keef is rumored to be picking up his regular show fee of $10,000. According to Schreiber, even at that per-song rate, Keef isn't the most expensive act on the bill today. "Not even close," he says, smiling and shaking his head. Between his concerts and purported three-million-dollar album deal, Keef, who dropped out of high school at 15, is on pace to out-earn President Obama in 2012.

If you do not know who Chief Keef is, you will soon. Last month, the South Side-born Keith Cozart signed a record deal with Interscope Records. The deal also included his life rights for a biopic, his own line of headphones ("Beats by Keef") and his own label to issue the records of other artists in his crew—effectively making him the youngest label head ever.

He became a phenomena via YouTube earlier this year with the low-budget video for "I Don't Like," a song chock full of bleak, misanthropic rhymes. It also features a few frames of the young rapper with a Glock in his grip—made all the more notable given that for the first half of the year he was on house arrest for a gun charge (he allegedly pointed a gun at a police officer).

Chief Keef is the prince of murder-capital Chicago rap, his insurgent popularity raising up the profiles of a dozen other local artists with him—a feat, given that it had been six years since the last Chicago rapper was signed to a major label deal. Since February, nine acts have announced their signings, with a handful of others in the works. Some, like King Louie, have already put years into developing their career. Others, like Lil Reese, have been signed off the strength of a verse and proximity to Keef. The last rash of outside interest in Chicago hip-hop that even broached this current level was roughly 15 years ago, when elder statesman Do or Die and Twista were fresh prospects.

Suddenly, where there was once no ladder up to the national spotlight and little evidence of an extant Chicago scene, there is a cottage industry of managers, labels and burgeoning talent putting the city on the map in a real way.

For Larry Jackson, the executive VP of A&R at Interscope who signed Keef, his initial reaction was visceral: "It scared me. And I knew it was going to be huge. It felt disturbingly powerful. Nobody really talks about Top 40 music anymore because the music is like wallpaper—it doesn't make you feel anything. ["I Don't Like"] pushes people."

Jackson says that the reason they gave Keef his own label was in order to grab any other Chicago talent that comes bubbling up. "We did it to widen the net—so that anything that comes within 50 feet of Keef, we can catch it." The label has already inked deals with two MCs who are part of Keef's crew, GBE. Lil Reese and Lil Durk both recently signed to Def Jam; Lil Durk was released this week after serving two months for a weapons charge.

For Interscope and the other labels that were courting him, Chief Keef's legal woes just added credibility to his swaggering image. While part of the appeal of this new wave of Chicago rappers is just that—the newness of it—hip-hop fans are eager to hear the real stories of the street, songs that are a true-to-life reaction to what's happening in America's murder capital. Keef's gun charge, for better or worse, adds authenticity to the biography he relates in his songs.

"You look at the news and see who is doing most of these killings—he fits that profile," explains Larry "Larro" Wilson, CEO of Lawless, the South Side record label that is home to King Louie and Katie Got Bandz. "Does it help that Keef is on house arrest? Absolutely."

For 18-year-old Tavares Taylor, who goes by the name Lil Reese, it all seems a bit unreal. He's know Keef since childhood and the two are still close; they have an air of brotherly collusion between them. Waiting backstage at Pitchfork, Reese's demeanor stands in stark contrast to Keef—while no less a talent, he still seems like a kid, unaffected and wowed by the attention. Up until two days ago, he didn't know what Pitchfork was or that it was even a big deal until he retweeted their review of his new mixtape and saw they have nearly 2 million Twitter followers. Backstage, he is listless, he wants pizza before he hits the stage but doesn't know where to get it; his manager J-Boogie presents him with the show contracts, which Reese signs atop a garbage can lid. The biggest difference between Keef and Reese is that Reese didn't expect this fame.

For Reese, the main thing that has determined his life and music is also the same thing he most wants to communicate to the rest of Chicago and the world. "I never felt safe. Still don't." J-Boogie arrives and begins herding the dozen-plus boys towards the stage, "It's time." Reese and Keef walk side by side in spotless head-to-toe white outfits, collars popped.

In these boys, Chicago has finally gotten the pop ambassadors it deserves—swaggering teenage wonders tapping into the zeitgeist like experts, telling their truth in blunt, steely lines. The first measure of "I Don't Like" booms and approx. 18,000 pairs of hands reach for the sky. The duo are met with screaming as they walk out from the wings. For the 10 minutes they are on stage, they are magnetic, Keef's incandescent—a natural—and suddenly they are done. Walking off stage, he finally agrees to be interviewed. Asked how it feels to have just played to his biggest hometown audience yet, he replies without pausing, "This? This ain't shit."

NUDE AWAKENING: SUICIDE GIRLS

SPIN magazine, February 2006

This piece was co-written and reported with my esteemed friend and colleague Julianne Escobedo Shepherd, who is gracious enough to let me include her work here.

"It's been blood, sweat and tears since the beginning," says Selena Mooney, as her blue eyes start to well up again. Mooney, 28, is better known as Missy Suicide, cofounder of SuicideGirls.com, the most visible alt-porn website on the Internet. As she sits in her office in SG's bubblegum-pink Los Angeles headquarters in mid-October, her soft voice is nearly drowned out by the din that accompanies her site's booming success, the constantly ringing phones and the clacking high heels of her all-female staff. On the wall behind her hang large color photographs of some of the site's most iconic women, all taken by Mooney herself. One of the portraits is of Katie, a short-haired brunette who was the site's first employee and later became its most visible model, and who just days earlier was named as a defendant in a lawsuit filed by SuicideGirls. In another image, a model name Sicily is clad only in a wet slip, her black-rimmed eyes cast heavenward; she left the company several weeks ago and has since become its loudest detractor. "The hardest part of this?" Mooney says. "Losing friends. Feeling betrayed and hurt."

The past month has clearly taken its toll on Mooney—not just the usual rigors of a 14-hours-a-day, six-days-a-week work schedule, but also the spate of behind-the-scenes troubles that have befallen her online enterprise. Beginning in September 2005, SuicideGirls weathered a series of allegations leveled by former models. More than 30 women have left since then, some claiming they had been subjected to unfair contracts and financial misdealings, others deriding the site's girl-positive brand image as a sham and complaining that they had suffered verbal abuse.

At the same time, SG was enjoying the biggest boom in its four-year history, thanks to a string of business deals that brought its instantly recognizable punk pinups to anyone who had cable TV, an iPod or a DVD player. In its expansion from a grassroots, online community to a multimedia corporation, SuicideGirls had garnered more than just name recognition. By the end of 2005, it was also involved in three different court cases and saw several disgruntled ex-models air their dirty laundry in the same types of online communities that SuicideGirls had helped pioneer. Now even the people who have been with the site since its inception are wondering if the idealism it was founded on has been lost. "We were beyond familial," says Mooney. "The girls expect a lot, and we tried to help. But when you grow, you lose innocence. You realize, reluctantly, how the world works."

When Mooney launched SuicideGirls in September 2001 with a male friend, Web developer Sean Suhl, she imagined the site as a more of an art project than an entrepreneurial venture. "My passion was taking pictures of these beautiful, strong women I knew," says Mooney, who was then a Portland, Oregon-based pinup photographer. "I was struck by the confidence they had in themselves and their bodies, and I wanted to share that confidence with the world." SG differentiated itself from mainstream porn by identifying itself as punk, offering its subscribers interactive bulletin boards, blogs and galleries of models who didn't represent the usual porn star aesthetic. "It didn't pander to pornography's idea of what sexy is," says author and sex educator Dr. Susan Block. "The women had wit and intelligence about them that was different from the traditional porn slut."

Slender, pretty, no-bullshit women who dig metal, grindcore and piercings, ex-models Jennifer Caravella (who still goes by her SG screen name Sicily) and Kelly Kleinert (who uses the nickname Shera) embody the archetype that has been integral to the site's success: hip, empowered young women who have no problem with getting naked or talking back. Kleinert, a 24-year-old college student from Reading, Pennsylvania, joined SuicideGirls in late 2002 because, she says, "I saw there were chicks like me there with tattoos, who seemed cool." Caravella, a 28-year-old performance artist from San Francisco, signed on a year later. And when the site kicked off a cross-country burlesque tour in May 2004, both women were selected to perform on it, each being paid $100 per show for a total of 41 dates. "There is definitely favoritism," Caravella says, "And once I joined the tour, I got to be a part of that more favored group of models."

The excursion is chronicled in the DVD *SuicideGirls: The First Tour*, a cheery travelogue that juxtaposes strip routines with *Real World*-style confessionals and scenes of the model causing jovial mayhem in punk clubs and EconoLodge parking lots. What the on-camera bonding doesn't reveal is the fear and doubt they were starting to feel about the site. "I was so excited about the whole tour," says Kleinert. "I was so eager to meet people I didn't realize it was weird the entire time."

Prior to the tour, SG cofounder Suhl had allowed some of the featured models in the film to live in the bottom-floor apartment of his sprawling home in Los Angeles' Los Feliz hills. While she and her tourmates rehearsed their choreography, Kleinert says, her interactions with Suhl were growing increasingly negative. "Sean can be the nicest guy," she says. "Sometimes I'd talk to him and think, 'I love this guy, he's going to do so much for me.' And then he turns on you in a second." By the time the girls hit the road, verbal attacks from Suhl had become a regular occurrence. "Sean would call the girls on the phone all the time, telling them to pull their performances together or they were off the tour," says Mike Marshall, the DVD's director. "I think he was trying to motivate them. It was stressful for [the girls] because they aren't professional dancers. There were growing pains." But the targets of Suhl's criticism saw it differently. "Every day was hell," says Kleinert. "Sean told us we sucked so much that we made this banner for our costume kit that said SUICIDE GIRLS BURLESQUE YOU SUCK."

Despite the instrumental role he plays in running SuicideGirls, Suhl remains an enigmatic figure. Before launching the site, the 30-year-old had survived the Internet bust of the 1990s to establish himself as an early proponent of Web communities and blog-based networks. He has become increasingly private since the onslaught of allegations (he declined to be photographed for this story and would only be interviewed by phone, reluctantly), ceding daily involvement and hands-on work to Mooney while concentrating on the site's development deals. The most personal information available on Suhl appears in his member profile on SuicideGirls.com, where he describes himself as "obsessive-compulsive, slightly agoraphobic," with a "fear of intimacy," and lists "McSweeney's stuff" and *Lolita* as some of his favorite reads.

Suhl maintains that his critiques of the burlesque shows were merely jokes. "I think if you asked some of the other girls, they would say it was funny, if you ask people who hate me now, they would say it was a horrible, demeaning, abusive act," he says. "There were still dinners bought, and people continued to live at the house, and it was all fine. Until they decided it wasn't fine."

Almost a year after the tour, in July 2005, Suhl allowed Caravella to move into his house. During her stay, Caravella claims, some of the models featured on *The First Tour* had grown increasingly concerned about receiving the 5-cent-per-disc royalty Suhl had promised them from DVD sales. (A publicist for SuicideGirls says that the women will be paid a royalty once the initial costs of the DVD are recouped.) Caravella says she asked Suhl to produce a contract: "I just wanted the piece of paper with his name on it that marks his word, that's all." But when she made the request, she says Suhl refused, then "flipped out." Shortly thereafter, he told her to move out, and Caravella quit the site.

Suhl doesn't deny kicking Caravella out of his house and counters that she had been taking advantage of him. "She came to me and said she had nowhere to live and nothing to eat," he says. "At the time, I did what I thought was right. I feel like taking in that person was a mistake. It wasn't a good situation."

This wasn't the first time Suhl had feuded with his models. Three years ago, Dia Mentia, a Web designer who posed in full-frontal photos wearing black lipstick and drizzling cherry juice over herself, became one of SuicideGirls' first models to have her own fan base. "I was SuicideGirls' cash cow," says the 30-year-old Mentia (who would only be interviewed on the condition that *SPIN* not publish a real name). But in January 2003, six months after she joined, Suhl asked her to leave the site, allegedly for disparaging other models on its message boards. "I shed no tears," she says. "I was like, 'If you're gonna kick me out, fuck you and I quit.'"

Mentia defected to another site, Deviant Nation, a punk-porn start-up that would have posed direct competition to SuicideGirls had it ever launched launched. In April 2003, SuicideGirls reported to the FBI that Deviant Nation's Chad Grant had hacked into SG servers; it also attempted to sue Grant in civil court, but when he didn't show up for the trial, SuicideGirls discovered it had sued the wrong Chad Grant—a different Californian with the same name. The debacle was later settled out of court. "The Chad Grant case was ludicrous," says Mentia. "Essentially, it was very specific to my leaving."

Two years later, the real Chad Grant would finally be charged by the FBI for the alleged hack. By then, however, he was just one more participant in an ever-expanding series of battles SuicideGirls was fighting, and Mentia would be there to chronicle them all. "Dia was only on the site for six months total," says Mooney, "but nobody has been as relentless" in attacking SuicideGirls. "At first, no one really listened to her. More recently, she seems to have found an audience."

While the alternative and online press were covering the release of *The First Tour*, they were also discovering two websites that had become clearinghouses for SuicideGirls-related complaints and gossip. Tales from the Darksite, a community on the blogging site LiveJournal, had become Mentia's forum to post updates about women who were quitting SuicideGirls, framegrabs of content that had been deleted from the models' blogs, and anything else she felt like ranting about.

GloomDolls.com, created by burlesque troupe manager Erin Oliver, published Caravella's long missives explaining her reasons for leaving the site, supplemented with supposed transcripts of instant-message chats between her and an explosive Suhl. "SG is not a feminist-empowered site," one of Caravella's statements read in part, "except that they have two frontwomen posing as spokeswomen. It's run by a man who is the only owner of the site, who's not progressive in his views on women. I'm being kind. I feel he's a raving misogynist and very ugly in how typical he is, though amplified and obviously a bit psychopathic. I and others who have known him feel the same."

Not all the information offered on the sites turned out to be truthful. Both Darksite and GloomDolls gave attention to a rumor that Suhl had kept models captive in his house, which he denies. "Depending on how you hear the story," says Suhl, "I'm either someone that beats up, rapes and locks girls in the basement, or I'm just someone who had a lot of hateful, untrue things said about them."

The websites were also used to publish business documents that models had to sign upon joining SuicideGirls, including, reportedly, the standard SG personal-release form. The one-page contract offers models a fee of $300 per shoot in exchange for granting Suicide-Girls "the exclusive, perpetual, and irrevocable right and license to copy, use and reuse, publish, distribute, edit, excerpt, exhibit, copyright and otherwise exploit model's image, picture likeness, persona, performance and voice in conjunction with the model's name, identification and related biographical information." Despite the severe language it uses, the contract may be essentially unenforceable. "The release is so poorly written that it is hard to say with any certainty what it means," says Barry Adler, a professor of contract law at New York University. "My take is that it was designed to give SG Services an absolute right to use and exploit, in any way, the images and recordings created by the models for the website. In any case, it would be ludicrous for the company to believe it could, with this release, forever stop the models from working on or profiting from other projects of any description."

Until recently, SuicideGirls limited the outside use of its models' images to promotional materials, banner ads, skateboard decks, the Playboy website and a photography book published in 2004. But in the summer of 2005, the site licensed the burlesque tour film to Showtime, which would air the documentary throughout the fall. The site also made SG videos available to iPod users (and yielded 500,000 free downloads in the first 24 hours they were available). Some models say they have no problem with this bargain. "We know our pictures will be used everywhere," says Reagan, a current SuicideGirl. "It's not their job to tell us where."

For others, the visibility was an unwelcome surprise. "I always thought fans of SuicideGirls would see the DVD and that's it—not that everyone and their mom was gonna see me on Showtime," says Kleinert. "I feel I got really screwed out of the deal. SuicideGirls keeps getting bigger, and I got nothing out of it, and it pisses me off."

In the two weeks after Caravella left SuicideGirls, Kleinert and original employee Katie Gilbert followed. Both Kleinert and Gilbert began modeling for God's Girls, another prospective SG competitor that promised similar-looking women but staked no claim to punk ideals. "I thought it would be fun to show alternative models in the same way we see the Pamela Anderson-types," says God's Girls founder Lara "Annaliese" Nielsen, 21, who refers to her site's financial backer, hardcore-porn magnate Gavin Lloyd, as "Uncle Gavin." "It would be quality photography with good makeup."

But their previous employers were determined to prevent them from appearing on competing sites. "The day I flew to L.A. for my God's Girl photo shoot," says Kleinert, "a packet of paper is sitting on [Nielsen's] doorstep saying if we did the shoot, SuicideGirls would sue." In fact, SuicideGirls had already filed suit against Nielsen and God's Girls, alleging violations of federal and state "unfair competition" laws, poaching models, and interfering with its business relationships. Gilbert, the onetime face of SG, had also been named in the suit for violating modeling and confidentiality agreements; the suit even claimed that God's Girls "features the same trade dress, including the use of pink as a primary color and the use of the stylized font utilized by SG." In a separate action, SuicideGirls sued Gloom-Dolls' Oliver, demanding that she apologize and turn over her website to SG. "The demands are ridiculous, and I would never adhere to them," Oliver says.

On September 27, 2005, the case of U.S. v. Chad Grant went to trial in a California court. Though Grant admitted to illegally setting up free SuicideGirls accounts and tampering with one aspiring model's online application, prosecutors were unable to prove that the site had suffered the damages it claimed. The case hinged on an $18,000 bill for repairs resulting from the hack issued by SuicideGirls' Web host, 3jane, a company that employs Suhl and is owned by his long-time friend Peter Luttrell. The trial ended in a hung jury, and a retrial is pending.

During the proceedings, SuicideGirls became fearful that images on its website depicting girls doused with fake blood and dressed in bondage gear would catch the attention of the FBI, so SG removed the images preemptively. "We got scared," says Suhl. "We all agreed that our business is not about bondage or blood. That's not the ethos of SuicideGirls or what we want to fight for. We took [those photos] down. It's not very punk rock and we know."

But some of its most vocal critics claim that the punk-rock spirit left SuicideGirls a long time ago and that punk porn is still porn, no matter how you qualify it. "They draw in girls who don't realize they're becoming a part of the sex industry," says Caravella. "It's sugar-coated. It's pink. It does not look like gross, nasty porn. It's not necessarily anyone's fault except mine for getting naked on the Internet."

Faced with the litany of troubles that SuicideGirls has endured over the past year, Suhl concedes that he may have instigated some of them, but he ultimately feels he's as much a victim as any of his models. "Honestly, I get bulldozed all the time," he says. "Those girls know how to work me; they know how to get what they want. But maybe I am intimidating. I feel like I give in, that I'm a sucker. Do you know what I mean by a sucker? You know, they give you the eyes, and they know how to talk you into things that sometimes aren't the most sensible."

In her pink office, Mooney says that the events of the previous year have made her more guarded and more reluctant to form friendships with people. But she prefers to concentrate on how the site's continuing expansion is helping to fulfill what she sees as Suicide-Girls' fundamental mission. "It's shocking to me that people are so focused on the negative and the gossip, when we are doing so many great things with the company," she says, pointing to future ventures that will see the SuicideGirls brand extended to comic books and clothing lines, and new businesses in Japan and Brazil. "It's very exciting that I can help another girl's art get into the hands of millions of people."

Without speaking the names of the women whose images still surround her every day, Mooney says their grievances are another natural outgrowth of SuicideGirl's rapid success. "There are going to be disgruntled employees," she says. "Some people need a scapegoat and want to blame someone else for their decisions." As much as she may wish circumstances were different, Mooney knows there are some things about SuicideGirls that even she can't change. "You can't be naive forever. It's a business now."

HOW SELLING OUT SAVED INDIE ROCK

BuzzFeed, November 2013

It's 2 p.m., the Friday before Christmas 2012, on the 21st floor of the Leo Burnett building in downtown Chicago. Young executives, creatives, admins and interns are all packed into a large meeting room, giddy and restless; today is special. Canadian sister duo Tegan and Sara step onto a foot-high stage and play three songs—including the first two singles from their seventh album, *Heartthrob*, which they will release the following month. The fluorescent lights stay on, the city's skyline splayed out behind them. Afterward, nearly all of the 200-odd employees in attendance will stand in line, phone at the ready, to pose for pictures with the band, just like fans after any concert.

Tegan and Sara, who eventually cracked the Top 20 with *Heartthrob*'s "Closer," need to win over this audience just as they would at any concert. A track in the right commercial could bring about the kind of attention that magazine covers and radio play alone can no longer garner. Commercial placement, also known as a "sync," has evidenced itself as the last unimpeded pathway to our ears—what was once considered to be the lowest form of selling out is now regarded as a crucial cornerstone of success. And as ads have become a lifeline for bands in recent years, the stigma of doing them has all but eroded. But with desperate bands flooding the market, the money at stake has dropped precipitously. Even the life raft has a hole in it.

"A tiny sliver of bands are doing well," says the duo's Sara Quin. "The rest of us are just middle class, looking for a way to break through that glass ceiling. The second 'Closer' got Top 40 radio play, we were involved in meetings with radio and marketing people who said, 'The next step is getting a commercial.' I can see why some bands might find that grotesque, but it's part of the business now."

Fifteen years ago, the music industry was still a high-functioning behemoth pulling in $38 billion a year at its peak, able to ignore the digital revolution that was about to denude it entirely. Starting in 1999, sales of recorded music fell an average of 8 percent a year; 2012 was the first time since then that sales went up—0.3 percent. Last year, it reported $16.5 billion in global revenue. America accounted for $4.43 billion of that—approximately the same amount spent by AT&T, Chevy, McDonald's and Geico on ad buys in the U.S. alone.

Back in the early '90s, when the music industry was thriving, commercials weren't a way indie bands got ahead—the punitive value outweighed the relatively small financial gains bands made for licensing a song to a commercial campaign. Band manager Howard Greynolds, who looks after the careers of Iron and Wine and Swell Season, was an employee at indie label Thrill Jockey when two of its flagship bands, Tortoise and Freakwater, each licensed a song for a 1995 CK One campaign.

"I remember people calling us saying, 'I can't fucking believe they did that, I can't support this band anymore!'" says Greynolds. "We were overly transparent then, we told people, 'Listen, this $5,000 bought them a van—*fuck off.*'" A few years later, another Thrill Jockey band, Trans Am, were outspoken about turning down a rumored $100,000 deal to license a song for a Hummer commercial. A generation ago, refusing these kinds of offers was a way for bands to telegraph where they stood, the sort of thing that showed their allegiance to the underground and their community.

It's been nearly 30 years since Lou Reed hawked Honda scooters with "Walk on the Wild Side" and 26 since Nike used (and was summarily sued for using) the Beatles' "Revolution" to sell sneakers, but the diminishing of outrage has sped up over the last decade. Volkswagen used Nick Drake's "Pink Moon" and a half-dozen Wilco songs, Apple placements are gold medals rather than albatrosses for relative newcomers like Feist and rock royalty like U2 alike, and no less an anti-commercialism scold than Pearl Jam got in bed with Target in 2009. Such moves are barely even press-cycle talking points by now.

Greynolds says what expedited this change wasn't just the huge drop in record sales, but as layoffs swept through the record industry, contacts from labels and distributors went to marketing, advertising and brands. "All of the sudden those were the people at music houses," says Greynolds. "People from your world. They might be feeding you a line of shit, but there was trust. They were different."

These new players within the advertising industry proved to be capable navigators of the ad world as well as the music underground. They could help forge lucrative connections between brands and cash-strapped bands—and their fan bases. Decades of posturing and sanctimony were rendered moot once artists realized that corporate gigs were the only paying gigs in town, a (very) necessary evil.

Sitting in his not-quite corner office, two floors below where Tegan and Sara played their lunchtime set, is the one of the most important gatekeepers of these coveted career-making opportunities: 38-year-old Gabe McDonough, Leo Burnett's vice president of music. Within the music industry, some believe McDonough and execs like him now play the role once occupied by major-label A&R guys—the talent seekers and overseers whose attention can mean the difference between music being your living or being your basement hobby. He handles everything from music supervision for commercials to pitching artists' tours for corporate sponsorships. His reputation was made early in his career for "breaking" Santigold with a Bud Light Lime spot and placing Brazilian pop oddities Os Mutantes in a McDonald's commercial—a spot that *AdWeek* named one of the five best uses of music in a commercial ever.

That was five years ago. McDonough's pre-agency cred originated as bassist in Chicago indie-rock band Boas (most of the band went on to form Disappears), and he's seen as a savvy translator between the creative and corporate sides. His most recent coup was getting Lorde's "Royals"—her first sync—for a Samsung campaign.

McDonough is effusive and modest, reluctant to claim credit for even the things he is often credited for. Tacked on the wall above his desk is a small slip of paper with a Warren Buffett quote: "It takes 20 years to build a reputation and five minutes to ruin it." Dressed in an anorak and expensive jeans, he looks as if he's in a successful Britpop band. On his desk are a stack of cassette tapes from a producer at a Los Angeles music house and a spray-painted vintage Walkman—a promotional item from another.

"Selling records was how [artists] made money," says McDonough. "With that gone, it's just never going to be the same. It's certainly not something that licensing music is going to remedy." But artists, labels and managers may beg to disagree: A one-year license for an existing song by a smaller band runs from $10,000–25,000, an original composition can run $25,000–30,000. A marquee-name band, for a year-long national campaign, could get $150,000 for existing work, or up to $300,000 for an original composition for a multi-year campaign. While licensing an album cut has the potential to break an album and make a career, 30 seconds of original music pays the same as months of intensive touring—and often anonymously.

"Five years ago, more bands said 'no,' but even five years ago, 'no' was the exception," says McDonough. "A band that turned me down five years ago just came in and played in our office last week." There are few bands that are no longer gettable; many are eager to take whatever money is on the table. Now when McDonough goes to a band with offers of whatever the client is interested in spending, "it's almost always 'yes.'"

McDonough insists that getting that perfect song into that right spot is a loose science at best. For a band that is teed up for such an opportunity—like Phoenix breaking through a Cadillac commercial, or fun.'s "We Are Young" in a Chevy Super Bowl spot—it can mean significant sales and radio play, as well as fast-tracking them to the mainstream. It shows they are an even more viable partner for brands. McDonough explains that the synthesis, when a song gets people talking about a commercial, cannot be manufactured. "You can't talk someone into, 'Strategically, this is the right piece of music for this spot.' The first thing people want is something that makes their commercial look great."

Though licensing a song to an ad is lucrative for an artist, McDonough says that the benefits of this relationship are even more valuable for a client. "Eight out of ten of the most-followed people on Twitter are musicians. Nine out of ten of the most-viewed things on YouTube are music videos. What's the value of having [a musician tweet] about something to 20 million followers? That's more than a primetime ad buy on NBC you could spend gazillions on. And musicians are finally starting to realize that this is worth more than any song [they] could write. *That's* money."

For bands and artists seeking commercial dough, the point of entry into the ad-world fray can come through music houses like Black Iris, which are commissioned by ad agencies to compose songs for their clients' campaigns. While the vast majority of music houses are standard-issue "jingle houses" that may draw upon pre-recorded libraries of music, there are approximately a dozen that posit themselves against the old stereotype. Comprising musicians who've come from bands in the independent music scene, they hire and/or license music from musicians who are from that same underground. Their stock is in being "music people" and their close associations—which cool scenes, producers and artists they have a connection to.

Daron Hollowell started Black Iris with two friends from Richmond, Virginia, after the demise of his band, 400 Years. Hollowell, 40, spent the early '90s sweating it out in basement shows on the hardcore circuit. For him, the revelation of doing commercial work was what it offered artistically. "There's the idea of writing something beautiful that somebody may never hear or [that may never] see the light of day—I don't know if that's any better than the other side of the scenario." Hollowell says he still has personal music projects on the side, but, "I'm not sure I'd want to be in a band, put a record out every year and a half, and go on tour. I have freedom from that."

Black Iris—as well as enterprises such as Heavy Duty, which boasts HAIM and Vampire Weekend producer Ariel Rechtshaid as a partner, and staff writers with songwriting credits on nine songs on Sky Ferreira's just-released debut album—has a cool cachet with ad agencies because of its ties to certain artists with which it works closely. It can offer entry to certain scenes and sounds companies want to transact with; many of the music houses also have other creative sidelines, for others, advertising work is the sideline. Black Iris has a singles label, White Iris; Hollowell admits to using this like a business card when meeting with ad creatives.

In a dark production suite in the Black Iris office, composer Rob Barbato is recording two demos for a commercial for a major national financial institution. An agency has commissioned original demos from Black Iris (and several other houses) for the spot. Barbato works quickly, switching between finessing a twee, acoustic pop track and a terse, synthetic one with a loop that mimics a boys' choir. After a few takes of whistling, his boss Hollowell pops his head in and interrupts—the singer they've hired for the spot is on her way over.

Prior to this, Barbato worked as a musician—first as a member of Darker My Love, later as Cass McCombs' sideman, and even doing a stint in The Fall. He went to Berklee College of Music, but instead of Barbato pursuing studio work like his classmates, Darker My Love got both a recording and a publishing deal. He quickly became uncomfortable, however, with the artistic compromises that were expected in exchange for advances the band was given. At 23, living on the road was his dream; by the time 30 rolled around, he wanted stability that touring couldn't provide and began working as a free-lancer for music supervisors Beta Petrol, before coming in-house at Black Iris last year.

"Everyone is constantly asking me about it," says Barbato of his musician friends, who are eager to commodify their songcraft at a higher rate than indie rock pays. He tries to help the ones who are genuinely interested whenever he can, but composing for commercials means being an engineer, dexterous composer and multi-instrumentalist—it's not for everyone. Barbato, and every producer and music supervisor interviewed for this story, says the common misconception is that writing music for commercials is easy because it's only 15 or 30 seconds of music, and musicians regard it as lesser art.

Other underground musicians are just happy to dabble—playing or singing on a demo for a spot can bring $100–200—though some older musicians and those with a particular DIY credibility still insist on keeping their names off of it. Barbato has done spots with members of bands whose names would be familiar to anyone who's read *Pitchfork* in the last five years, who take pains to keep their corporate toil anonymous. Barbato understands that, but he's emphatic that to differentiate between commercial music and indie rock is to draw a line that does not exist; it's simply a matter of degrees.

"If someone in the independent-rock world thinks that this is bullshit, they should take a look at themselves. They're doing the same thing; they're writing albums that people stream 30 seconds of on fucking *Pitchfork* and then people are like, 'Oh, I like your album.'"

The real difference between a preening, indie-rock band and a commercial composer is that Barbato is pulling down a low six-figure paycheck annually, and he still has the freedom to entertain purely creative pursuits like producing albums. Aside from his salary, Barbato gets royalties if his original composition makes it into a client's spot. When he was a freelance composer, if a spot made it into a national ad, he'd net a few thousand bucks—more than he ever made playing in successful bands. Some of Black Iris' core staff originated in the Richmond hardcore scene; almost all of its employees and freelancers—including members of Fool's Gold, Eric Pulido of Midlake, and Andy MacFarlane of the Twilight Sad—still play and tour in bands.

Barbato is setting up the studio to track vocals with a female singer, a known-name solo artist in indie rock. She's done demo work for Black Iris periodically and is looking to get back into it; she's broke until her album comes out this fall. (She asked not to be identified.) Though she is signed to a prestigious indie label with worldwide distribution, she's barely scraping by and has been saying yes to whatever opportunities arise. Today, it's harmonizing on a bank commercial for $100 while in Los Angeles to play Coachella.

She curls up on the black leather sofa in the control room and Barbato plays her the track a few times so she can pick up the melody. "So, kind of a Shins-y thing?" she asks. He nods. The song is sweet, pretty, California folk pop, with a little ukulele. If stretched to song length, it'd be getting raves from music sites for being so instantly memorable.

Barbato sets her up with a mic in the neighboring tracking room and the singer runs through her clarion *aahs* a few times until she nails it. Barbato gets a few takes and gives her the thumbs-up. They got it.

Lunch arrives, and Barbato, Hollowell and the singer catch up over their salads. She's put her stuff in storage, she's trying to figure out what she's doing with her life and her career. She's tried her hand doing freelance composition for spots—the money for that work is better—but she admits she doesn't fully have the knack for it; composing often involves quickly revising a piece of music several times to meet a client's specifications. She is eager for session work like this, which is easier for her to fit into her schedule.

On her way out the door, the singer asks, "So, should I just invoice you then?"

"Yeah," says Hollowell.

She flashes a big smile and reminds them of her availability for next week before she waves goodbye. Neither track would ultimately wind up being awarded the spot; the client ended up licensing a pre-existing track from another artist.

Beta Petrol's founding partner Bryan Ray Turcotte is perhaps the ultimate poster child for outré artists seeking credit in the straight world. The small firm specializes in music supervision for film, TV and commercials, and Turcotte is known to be one of the foremost punk collectors in the world, having amassed a stunning amount of memorabilia, art and ephemera. On display in his office is a Cannes Lion he won for a Nike spot, as well as the original mold for Devo's flowerpot hats.

Turcotte is author of best-selling punk-art tome *Fucked Up + Photocopied*, and the Beta Petrol office houses two employee-run labels—one issues vinyl only, the other cassettes. Turcotte's meeting immediately prior to this interview was with Gee Vaucher of British anarchist-punk heroes Crass about a series of exhibitions Turcotte is curating with the Los Angeles Museum of Contemporary Art. Beta Petrol's ad-world business is tangled in its creative endeavors, serving as the money hose for artistic pursuits. But Turcotte knows commercial work is the only lifeline some bands have and sees it as a way to help keep artists going for another album, another tour.

When Turcotte started out 12 years ago, many artists considered commercial work to be gauche, but a big part of the problem, says Turcotte, was the (corporate) messenger. "They don't know how to talk to DIY artists about what it means," he says. "It was just, 'We want your song in perpetuity.'" It was a natural place for Turcotte, a former musician, to serve as a go-between.

"It was an uphill battle. Some bands were not going to do it at all." Over time, Turcotte found bands that would. Then it was a matter of working the corporate side to finesse the licensing rights, whittling terms down to what was actually needed rather than blanket licenses. The next steps were unconventional work-arounds; Turcotte would often circumvent managers, publishers, and labels—people who had a piece of the artists' pie—in order to appeal directly to an artist about why the spot was right for them. (Turcotte once called Lou Reed at home about use of two Velvet Underground songs; the ploy worked.) And all of this was fueled by a Robin Hood philosophy that is, in its own way, punk rock.

"I got into the business to put the money where it should be—in artists' hands," says Turcotte.

"It was more money than we made in a year," says Matt Johnson of Matt and Kim, a band born of Brooklyn house shows, explaining that their advertising windfall also gave them a mainstream career along the way.

Before that, the duo, who are a couple, were touring constantly and hovering around the federal poverty line. Though they had trepidation about what doing a commercial would mean, it was limited to fear of backlash from within the DIY scene of which they were a part. In 2008, they'd licensed "Yea Yeah" for a Virgin Mobile campaign; negative reaction was limited to a few Myspace comments. The following year, when Beta Petrol wanted their single, "Daylight," for a Bacardi spot, the duo's initial impulse was to take the money and run.

"We thought, maybe no one would ever see the ad, or even recognize the song," says Johnson. The money would buy them a van, though it was enough to have bought them a house. They said yes, and quickly began to regard it as much of a Matt and Kim commercial as a Bacardi one. "I have a gold record for that song, and it wouldn't be here if it had never aired."

For some artists, taking a check from Bacardi, Pepsi or Red Bull is an easier transaction than dealing with labels in that it's cut-and-dry—everyone knows what they're getting.

"What artists need are resources to make music, go on tour, make videos, grow their networks and expand their audience," explains Adam Shore, who manages Best Coast, who have soundtracked commercials for Windows, Payless and J.C. Penney (and recorded their debut album at Black Iris' studio.) While bands need the same things they always have, record labels are at a loss for how to create revenue and provide reach. Larger deals (and larger advances) come at the expense of selling off an artist's rights to everything—publishing, merchandising, tour revenue.

Meanwhile, a commercial sync has more reach, nominal terms and bigger paydays. If ad execs are the new A&R, then it only serves that brands are the new record labels, yet "brands can provide these better than labels ever could, at minimal cost and effort to them," says Shore. "Plus, they don't want to own your albums."

Turcotte explains it this way: "You can be very successful being a small band that has control of its destiny versus a bigger band that has to answer to a [record label]." Compared with record deals, which have become insidious and vast as labels seek greater dominion in order to profit, licensing a song for a beer commercial is practically free money. It's a choice at a time where options are rare. "When we started, you could control where your music was or wasn't," says Quin, "but now that feels impossible."

In recent years, as bands and managers have seen that ads can be a proven method of discovery for new artists, it's become much easier for Turcotte to get songs. "I'm seeing baby bands talk about advertising the way that baby bands used to talk about getting signed, which is very interesting to me," he says. "It's like the in-house music producers are the new A&R guys, and the bands want an ad, just the way they wanted a record deal. That's what they aspire to have. And that's something I could have never expected because I never thought that it would have that much power."

The evolution has also happened within the business itself. A song can put nuance to a brand identity; an artist's identity—what their art has made us believe about them and why—can be just as easily loomed to a product. That has long been understood, but perhaps what has evolved since "I'd Like to Buy the World a Coke" went from soda-pop jingle to *Billboard* Top 10 pop single is just how much meaning a band, a song and their fan base can impart in this co-signing.

Johnson admits that while syncs are how Matt and Kim make their living now, he is mindful of corporate credibility—the duo recently turned down a spot for a breakfast product (the spot ran with a song composed to sound nearly identical) as well as spots that a friend's band later said yes to. What won't they do? "Yogurt," says Johnson. "Cheesy commercials with the mom—it's not artistic. We'd have a hard time keeping our edge as a band."

Almost a year after Tegan and Sara played their Leo Burnett lunchroom gig, they've finally landed their first national spot—stemming from a different agency gig they did this past summer, placing "Shock to Your System" in a JBL campaign that begins in November. Some within their promotions team are worried that after all this effort, a commercial spot that introduces an album track won't be the thing that seals the deal. Says Quin, "If people can't connect that song to you—your name, your face—then it's all for naught."

Still, McDonough is emphatic that even a saturated market is better than nearly any option an artist could have: "Ads are not the answer; it's just a piece of the puzzle." Now that so many bands are trying to get their piece of it, the value on sync licenses have come down. ("*Way* down," he clarifies.) The trend is away from original compositions and toward existing tracks, which are always cheaper. "Two decades ago, there was crazy money," McDonough says. "The money now is not life-changing for anyone."

For all the freedom and choices an infusion of ad money can provide, or the signal boost a well-placed spot can provide, it comes at a cost. Success can change things, just as sure as a platinum record once did, and access to lump sums can affect which direction a band is facing as a corporate client becomes the only paying audience they have.

While advertising cannot save or replace the music industry, there is one undeniable fact, says McDonough: "These big companies are the last people paying musicians what they are worth."

NOT LOLLAPALOOZA: ROLLIN HUNT, SCREAMING FEMALES & ABE VIGODA

Chicago Reader, August 2007

This weekend the throngs will decamp for Lollapalooza to experience a vertiginous array of mediocre-to-terrible bands (and a couple good ones) in the company of tens of thousands of half-drunk strangers. Seeing a show outside in the Chicago summer dusk is a welcome reprieve from standing around in a smoky club, but the idea that mega-festivals somehow create ad hoc communities out of their mega-crowds—a meme we probably owe to Woodstock—is ridiculous. The only thing everybody at Lollapalooza has in common is the willingness to be painfully gouged for a ticket. Even crowds that might seem a bit more like-minded (say, at Pitchfork) make for a grim and dystopian scene: mini mountains of litter, security guards, sun-baked Porta-Johns. And when you see bands from hundreds of feet away, they seem unreal—specks on the horizon, or larger-than-life cartoons rendered in Jumbotron pixels and playing hard to the cameraman.

As much as I love being able to eat funnel cake and watch M.I.A. at the same time, it can't make up for all the things about festivals that are fundamentally wack. This summer I've made it my mission to forsake the colossus for basement shows, hoping to find exciting new bands and join their tiny fan base.

The first time I saw local songwriter Rollin Hunt, he was wowing a crowd of a dozen or so at Ronny's, trembling before the mic with his eyelids squeezed shut. "Wow. He's really special," I whispered to my friend. "Yes," she said. "Very." Hunt was in the middle of a song about going out for a walk and spying on a couple getting hot and heavy in their bedroom. And antelopes.

Onstage, Hunt is terminally shy, like he's cowering from his own voice—it seems like he's used to doing this sort of thing in private. His small, crackly vocals and the songs' ramshackle instrumentation constantly get away from each other. For me, the mystery of Rollin Hunt is whether he's oblivious to how wide off the mark he's gone. Is he on this strange path by conscious choice, or did he simply pursue his love for the Beach Boys and '60s girl groups and just happen to produce his savant-garde doo-wop? His work is so beautifully awkward that it's hard to believe it's all part of a deliberately-crafted persona.

Hunt's self-released ten-song demo, *Dearly Honorable Listener*, is closer to outsider art than lo-fi indie rock. It's a marvel of rawness, recorded so poorly that you have to turn your stereo almost all the way up to hear what's going on—you get about 60 percent background hiss and 40 percent music. Live, Hunt is often accompanied by a shambling little backup band, but on disc it's just him, his not-quite-in-tune guitar, and sometimes a drum machine. (At least I think it's a drum machine—often it sounds like someone throwing rocks into a bucket.) The songs begin and end in strange places, like he either ran out of tape or started playing without telling whoever was supposed to press the record button. He has a hard time keeping up with the drum machine, which sometimes drops in jarringly in the middle of a verse, and he multitracks vocal harmonies through what sounds like a baby monitor.

Hunt's ambition as a performer nearly destroys his sweet, fragile little tunes, mostly because it completely outstrips his basic competence—but they end up amazing anyway. His lyrics are crowded with small scenes and unpredictable tangents: one song is about "juice in the air," another about "George who runs the Holiday Inn." His genius turn is "Pamphlet," where he proposes a solution to his relationship problems in a romantic ditty that sounds like a cross between early Smog and a truly touched Frankie Lymon: "I need to make you / A pamphlet / That tells you everything you need to know / About my feelings." It's clunky, unpolished, and intimate, and that's what gives it its magic.

When Screaming Females hit Ronny's in mid-July, they had a paying crowd of six. I'm not counting the people in the other band or the sound guy, who was playing Tetris on his cell phone. They were halfway through a two-and-a-half-month U.S. tour with stops at plenty of basements and punk spaces—a few days earlier they'd played a house show in Elgin. But though these three under-20 kids from New Jersey are almost entirely unknown, word is spreading fast. Frontwoman Marissa Paternoster is the teenage girl-guitarist messiah, and miracles and conversions come with the territory—

show by show, she's turning the uninitiated, myself included, into true believers.

We may be witnessing the dawn of a new age of femme shredders (Marnie Stern, Aimée Argote of Des Ark), but Paternoster isn't waiting around to see if anyone else is following her. On a defiant, punk-fast version of Neil Young's "Cortez the Killer," she carved into the song until practically the whole thing was a solo. Screaming Females have just self-released their second album, *What If Someone Is Watching Their TV?*, and it can match any (decent) Dinosaur Jr. record, pound for pound, in teen malaise and ripping solos. Paternoster's got some blues boogie in her riffing, a little Billy Gibbons in her muscular punk. She's a deft songwriter, but she doesn't like to let more than a minute or two go by without stepping on a stomp box and firing one off. She ended the set in a cloud of screeching feedback, hunched over her guitar and pounding on her pedals with her fists. I don't think anything like her has happened to punk before, and I'm glad it finally has.

Two weeks ago, the posi-kidcore band Abe Vigoda brought L.A.'s Evolution Summer scene to a pair of Chicago basements: the first night they shimmified 19 stinky kids and a beer-drunk dog at a party in Pilsen, and the second they did a last-minute set at People Projects as the token dudes at a Ladyfest benefit, playing for maybe 20 people, half of them festival volunteers. In Pilsen, they kept it short and sweet, with six songs in less than 15 minutes: "We've gotta make it quick before the cops show back up," explained guitarist/chatterbox Juan Velazquez. The PA kept feeding back and you couldn't hear the singing, so the band turned off the mics and just shouted along—none of us really knew how the songs went anyway, and everyone was too busy dancing to care.

The B side of Abe Vigoda's recent "Animal Ghosts" seven-inch, "All Night and Day," hasn't left my turntable since I dropped it on. Their tribal thunk and sideways funk make for a kind of dance punk nobody else has dreamed up yet. Full of jostling guitars that manage to be both precise and playful, their sound has a kind of cloistered innocence—it knows nothing of disco. Calypso would be more like it, given the deep love these guys have for the woodblock. Abe Vigoda's antecedents are hard for me to pin down—maybe dub, maybe New Zealand pop, maybe some band they hang out with in Chino that I don't know about—but no matter how you slice it, their show is a cynicism-destroying good time.

We're supposed to believe that we're enjoying some sort of meaningful collective experience at a big festival, with modern rock blaring from a bank of speakers the size of a condo complex. But such a grand scale actually tends to dissolve community—the anonymity and impersonality of an enormous event sometimes even encourages people to act shittier than they otherwise would, since they don't feel accountable to anyone around them. At a basement show, though, where the bands aren't whisked to the stage by golf carts to make a thousand dollars a minute, people are gonna get pissed if you leave your chewed-up corn cobs and beer cups lying around. You can smell the band. You can give them seven bucks for a T-shirt and know that the money is going to get them a tenth of the way to Iowa City. In the basement, you can feel the band's humanity as well as your own.

PART
EIGHT

FEMALES

ST. VINCENT: *STRANGE MERCY*

Village Voice, **November 2011**

Annie Clark is too perfect a rock star, but she will do. She has china doll features; she is put-together and glamorous; her manner is refined. She's beautiful, and you can tell she is used to being looked at and watched, as if she has been famous since long before now.

Looking at her when she's offstage, you imagine she should be doing something else, not staying up late with a guitar slung 'round her back and commanding a band into loud swells of her own design. It seems like the wrong job for her hands. She seems more coquettish than rock and roll as she's curled up on the couch backstage before her show in her emerald crepe dress.

When Annie Clark gets onstage as St. Vincent, her image is mere collateral. What fixes your gaze to her is the confidence, the ease, and the naturalness she exudes. You cannot imagine she was meant for anything else but stomping around the stage, coaxing new noise from her guitar, her eyes surveying the sold-out crowd. She solos; they scream.

"I'm not qualified to do anything else," she says, sounding a little concerned—as if she had been browsing Craigslist ads for admin positions while casting about for a post-Berklee-dropout plan B. "I didn't think I needed it. Which sounds insane when I say it aloud."

It's not. It's only reasonable. Clark's third record, *Strange Mercy*, is her best and most pop album. The signs of her success are ample. For one thing, *Mercy* sold 20,000 copies in its first week of release. Still, she plays modest, or at least presents as the anti-diva—"It would be interesting to know exactly how many people have heard my songs," she says. Her guess: "Like, 100,000?" Perhaps that would be the case if everyone who'd bought a copy of her last few albums had kept them entirely for themselves, she'd never toured, filesharing didn't exist, and her songs weren't presently all over radio and the blogosphere.

With *Strange Mercy*, Clark moves closer to her audience, lowers the transom a bit. On her previous two albums, *Marry Me* (2007) and

Actor (2009), it was hard to tell what, if anything, was personal. Her debut seems to be made up of vignettes and stories. She cited "Pirate Jenny" and Nick Cave as her inspirations for its theatricality. It seemed the work of someone eager to impress—to show off, even. *Actor*, purportedly a tribute to Clark's favorite films, resulted in Clark rhapsodizing over Woody Allen's work as much as explaining her own. She says of her progress as a songwriter since: "I care less about impressing. Well...maybe. It's no longer about trying impress people with my wit."

Audiences want confessional bits from rock icons, and expect them from female singer-songwriters. Clark doesn't give them up easily, but *Strange Mercy* is being called "candid." The singer is still cagey, though there is discernibly more of her on here. Was it intentional?

"Was I trying to be candid? Hmm." She munches an apple and considers what to say. "I want to give you answers, but I am also aware this is to be printed in a magazine, so I'm at a bit of an impasse. But I don't want to give you a rote answer, though that rote answer is quite true. There are songs here that are very, actually, candid. But I won't say which those are."

Although she hemmed over making her art more personal, the candor came naturally, which she characterizes as scary. She didn't have as much time or ability to dress up or intellectualize what was coming out of her, so some songs remained as visceral as they were when initially written. "2010 was a rough year. Tough stuff. Rough time. When life was actually hard, I had less time to wring my hands about music. It got to be what it should be, a great thing—a replenishing thing." She adds, apologetically, "Not to use a spa word."

Much has been made of the album closer, "Chloe in the Afternoon," which is somewhere between "Afternoon Delight" and Anaïs Nin, lyrically; it depicts soft sadism with a girl in a hotel room. Is Clark put off by how this one song has resulted in people calling *Strange Mercy* "sexual"? "It's not like I should have called the record *'Get Down to Fuckin,'*" she laughs. "I think people focus on something like that because it's titillating." Given that female performers often have their work sexualized, regardless of whether their work is sexual or not, was she hesitant to make a song so blatantly erotic? "I was more reluctant to write a song about that power/sex/domination trifecta, that murky water where it all swims around together," she says. "That felt more complicated than it being about something sexual."

If there is a theme to be found on *Strange Mercy*, it involves dissolving an identity, or another person's idea of that identity. Clark's modesty is belied by her awareness of and use of her own image—as a beautiful woman, as a gossamer shredder of skill and confidence, as a woman in charge of her career, as a popular singer of pop songs. She knows what she is working with. She understands the machinations of fame, of why her audience likes (and loves) her; she is careful but solicitous enough with the press that pokes at her. "I have one answer for you if the tape recorder is on, and another if it's off," she says when asked about her awareness of her own image. "That's my answer there."

Still, Clark says she feels like a fraud much of the time. "It's complicated to exist in the world—everyone feels that, whether or not you have a modest amount of notoriety," she says. "I was reading this Miranda July piece in *The New Yorker*, and it ends with a line about how feeling like an adult also means feeling like a fraud. I think if anyone has any kind of self-awareness, they've felt like a fraud—with other people or in relationships. I feel that way. And maybe it's more powerful to put that out there. To just own that, then to keep being, like, 'Watch me sing and dance, I've got all the bases covered, don't worry.'"

The singer's measured control seems to keep her from truly letting it all (or, even, some of it) hang out. She credits her politeness to her mother, whom she describes as a saint, and to her cultural inheritance as a Texan. She says she learned the value of professionalism from her aunt and uncle, the folk duo Tuck & Patti, whom she toured with as a teen. "It's not the '80s or the '90s anymore; it's not a gravy train," she says of the music business. "If you want to have a career for a long time, you need to act right. I know it's counterintuitive to the whole rock 'n' roll thing, but I have never acted like I was a person who was so unimpeachably great that I could afford to be an asshole to people, nor would I want to be. I take it seriously."

To be a rock star involves more than just charisma, or good songs, or talent (talent usually least of all). One must be a capable player and have an appealing image—and, perhaps, most of all, a clear confidence that one deserves to be in front of an audience. In that regard, Annie Clark is a natural-born rock star; she just happens to be working below the arena radar. She doesn't disagree. "There are plenty of things I am not confident about, but *this* I can do."

CAT POWER: *SUN*

SPIN magazine, September 2012

Chan Marshall insists that her ninth album isn't political, but in America in 2012, what's more politicized than the right to live as you please? *Sun* is hardly sloganeering, but its Power to the People ruminations are more potent and topical than you'd expect from a pop record—and certainly one made by Cat Power.

You'd think a polemic dispatch from the thick of Koch Brothers-fuelled culture war might result Cat Power hitting new depths of emotional dispossession, but lo! Marshall instead loses some of her famous ethereal malaise and conjures vampy disdain. There is a power to it; it is empowered. Which pushes *Sun* away from the rest of her discography (*Moon Pix*, for example), in that Marshall now sounds engaged with the pain of the world, no longer a mere interpreter of (her own) malady. Even her most joyous album, *The Greatest*, seemed to amount to stylized pain with the doomed singer as a medium, a conduit harmed by all that she was divining. No one expected valedictory rebirth—'specially her, as she implies on opener "Cherokee," that if her time here is cut short, it will be by her own hand, given her request to be buried upside-down—an 18th-century practice to prevent suicides from haunting the earth. Touching on her own mortality before she hits her album's second verse is the only predictable Cat Power move Marshall makes here.

But that life-or-death bit isn't morbidity so much as candor. *Sun* sheds the myopia inherent in depression; Marshall repeatedly insists that she's here, with us, and it feels like a revelation. It's a Mary J. Blige power position, self-assured and strong (the first line of "Cherokee" quotes the Missy Elliott-penned "Never Been," from Blige's *No More Drama*). What we get is not so much a new Cat Power as the true Cat Power: She's been to the brink and emerged on the other side to share her testimony. Akin to her profligate Miami neighbor Rick Ross on his own latest, Marshall is showing us her consciousness, her empathy—if her tears are there, they're on the inside.

This record is more about "you" and the collective "we," and on "Human Being," she attempts to shred the distance between "them" and "us": "See the people on TV / Get shot in their very own street / People just like you, people just like me." The album's denouement, "Nothin But Time," opens with a similar I-feel-you salvo:

I see you, kid, you got the weight on your mind
I see you're just trying to get by

Heart-heavy but with her hope still afloat, she affirms and names the kid's pain; it's a different kind of vulnerability than what we're used to from her. Later, she sings, "Never never give up what you always wanted / Never ever give in," and the *you*'s turn to *I*'s. She caps the song ecstatically, bellowing "I wanna live!" alongside Iggy Pop, but nine songs in, she'd already disabused us of any doubt.

Musically, *Sun* is a new trick for Marshall as well. A tribute to her belief that contemporary R&B has the power to salve, the self-produced album's sound is closer to the street and further from the bedroom. There is still some guitar (Marshall's lead on "Cherokee", the Judah Bauer-sampling "Ruin"), but the record is driven by synths-and-drums slinkiness, Marshall's attempt to mimic the contemporary Top 40 hip-hop and soul records she loves. And though it's still probably best qualified as "indie"—as it is not crystalline and Katy Perry-fied—it possesses none of the sonic modesty that tag usually shorthands. It's closer to Gaga than Grimes, but no less for it's allegiances. "Ruin" builds on a house-y piano 8, and then explodes into a disco-Stones vamp. Finally, a Cat Power song you can dance to.

Elsewhere, *Sun*'s title track could work as the plot synopsis for Lars von Trier's *Melancholia*; on "Ruin," she "wants out / Want on my own," and follows that up with "Always on My Own," which is more a dirge-y interlude than a song, the titular sentiment delivered more as a statement of fact than a complaint. The album's one throwaway is "3,6,9," notable for its Ying Yang Twins quotation: The lyrical "monkey on my back" cliché is beneath her, and anyway, fans tend to over-marvel whenever an indie darling even acknowledges hip-hop, though Marshall's been a vocal proponent for years. (She's probably listening to some lesser DJ Khaled posse cut as you read this.)

Speaking of which, album closer "Peace and Love" has the same locomotive chug as her beloved Jay-Z's "99 Problems," but in treacle-time with minor chords, though her Hova-esque, rags-to-riches ambition suggests she's harder than we think: "I'm a lover but I'm in it to win," she crows, lest you mistake someone with nine albums as unmotivated. On the quite perfect single, "Ruin," she tacitly tackles first-world privilege, quasi-rapping (!) a range of far-flung locales she's visited—"Dhaka / Calcutta / Soweto / Mozambique / Istanbul"—over a swift 4/4 stomp, before returning to God Blessed America, where people are "bitchin', moaning" despite the fact that "some people ain't got shit to eat." It's the sort of sneering indictment you expect from M.I.A., not the woman who wrote the louche's anthem "Lived in Bars."

But *Sun*'s absolute standout is "Manhattan," a quiet meditation on the island's pre-9/11 meaning, with the Statue of Liberty framed as the metaphorical woman behind a successful Man(hattan), a beacon of freedom that lures people from all over America (and the world) with the promise that you can be who you want to be here. It's subtler than patriotism; the abstraction is a nostalgic ruing for that old-fashioned American freedom (not the 2012 GOP's hijacked late-stage-capitalism-amok-in-your-uterus version), the sort that might entice a young girl to move up from Georgia with just a lamp, a chair and her guitar.

This is the album's heart, with Marshall cooing her thrall for the moon that hangs above the city over a soft, motorik beat: "Liberty in the basement light / Free speech / Lipstick in the moonlight." It's liberty as we learned it in school: The chance to live the life of your secret dreams, unencumbered by who you were in another town, a different life, to come to this place where freedom is so free you can take it for granted. The song is full of sweetness and a knowing sadness, and it's one of the finest Marshall's ever written.

Recent Cat Power profiles and early *Sun* reviews take pains to mention a recent breakup with a bold name that happened three years after this self-guided, self-recorded odyssey of Marshall's began; we've made assumptions, despite her insistence that *Sun* isn't a breakup album. (Said assumptions are forgivable, of course: Soft agony has been her idiom since the '90s.) But it's clear that her years spent bringing this record into the light—perfecting her own drumming so she could sample it, building songs bit by bit from the eagle drop on "Cherokee" to the chinging castanets on "Peace and

Love"—made her vision that much stronger. Marshall has admitted she wept when someone at Matador told her the album's early demos sounded like "old, sad Cat Power." You can hear the fight to be understood, to show us not who she was, but who she is: a free woman in Miami, to misquote Joni Mitchell, fettered and alive. *Sun* is a spirited violation of what we think we know about her, content to show us a different kind of discontent.

SWF, 45: MECCA NORMAL'S
THE OBSERVER
Chicago Reader, **April 2006**

Mecca Normal's new album, *The Observer*, is hard to listen to. Not for the usual reasons—it doesn't suck. What makes it tough going is the same thing that makes it great: subtitled "A Portrait of the Artist Online Dating," it's so mercilessly personal it's hard to believe it can exist in the pop-music marketplace, let alone anywhere outside of a diary. A concept album about Jean Smith's romantic life as a single woman of 45, it develops a grim, intimate picture of the solitary struggle for connection that doesn't go easy on anyone—not Smith, not the men she dates and certainly not the audience.

The pop canon is full of songs about romantic longings and failures, so that we've been conditioned to expect certain story arcs, delivered in each genre's codified language—blues and its backdoor men, contemporary R&B and its baby boos, classic rock and its lonely motel rooms. There's pleasure in having our sufferings and hopes reaffirmed, however approximately, by such archetypes. But Mecca Normal, the Vancouver duo of Smith and guitarist David Lester, have spent two decades hammering away at musical and social convention. They're overtly political artists—anarchist-feminists both, they've developed a traveling workshop called "How Art and Music Can Change the World"—and their loose, abrasive, drumless songs don't rest easily in any genre. And even coming from them, *The Observer* is startling.

When we listen to music it's natural to try to relate to the singer's experience or inhabit it as our own, but getting invited along on Smith's blind dates and hookups is discomfiting to say the least—as a storyteller, she skips the niceties and just plunks everything down on the table. "He tries to put the condom on / He curses / I try to see what he is doing," she sings in her low, acidic croon. "But I'm pinned beneath him / I hear him stretching the condom like he's making a balloon animal."

All but a couple of the album's 12 songs are connected to its basic theme of relationships between the sexes, and half are diaristic syn-

opses of actual dates Smith went on with men she met at Lavalife.
com. She's a sharp, literate lyricist, prosaic rather than melodic—
right now she's at work on her fourth novel—and her attention to
detail and detached, acerbic tone make *The Observer* a particularly
apt title. Though each diary song is a separate scene, with each man
allowed his own particulars, they're unified by Smith's blunt por-
trayal of herself—we learn about her as a date, not just an artist, and
she makes a messy, inconsistent impression, veering from cynical
and judgmental to petulant and needy.

On the album's centerpiece, the 12-minute "Fallen Skier," she skips
between snippets of dinner conversation and an internal monologue about her date, a 47-year-old student and recovering addict
who describes himself as a "fallen waiter/ski bum/party guy." From
the moment she says "guy," drawing it out and accenting the word,
you can tell she's mocking him. She repeats his story without sym-
pathy, sounding frustrated, almost disgusted: "I feel I'm with a boy,
a very young boy / He's only been away from home for 27 years /
Only 27 summers, 27 winters / Partying and skiing / I guess that's
why he hasn't gotten anything together yet / I don't think he re-
alizes it, but his life has gotten away from him." When he seems
concerned that her band might play hardcore punk, she makes a
half-indignant aside that lightens the mood: "I stand, a middle-aged
woman in a fantastically subtle silk jacket / Hush Puppies / Curly
hair blowing in the wind / And this guy's fretting over the possibility / That I'm actually Henry Rollins." But almost immediately
her complaints begin to boomerang, telling us as much about her as
they do about him. "He never asked the name of my band," she says,
"never tried to touch me." Suddenly she sounds vulnerable, even
wounded; though her date's clearly wrong for her, she can't keep
herself from wanting to be interesting and desirable to him. When
she hugs him good-bye at the end of their chemistry-free evening,
it's unclear which one of them she's trying to console.

The Observer is a harsh toke, but it's compelling on all fronts—Smith's
lyrics force you to think about loneliness, need and bad dates, but
the songs are as engrossing as they are exhausting. Her voice flits
and dips like a plastic bag in the wind, moving from a moany sort
of sung-speech to a deep, silky quaver to a thick, shrill trilling, and
she often drawls out her words like she's trying to fill the room with
distended consonant sounds. The self-explanatory album opener,

"I'm Not Into Being the Woman You're With While You're Looking for the Woman You Want," is a glowing example of the interplay between her vocals and Lester's guitar, which is equally distinctive and powerful. On "To Avoid Pain" the duo toys with early-'60s pop country as Smith hee-haws like a half-drunk Brenda Lee, trying to talk herself down on the way to a first-time hookup: "Take a city bus / To a downtown hotel / I don't feel weird / I don't feel weird / Ask me / Ask me / Ask me if I do." Then, as a dark, discordant synth tone rises out of the music, she eagerly proclaims a dubious victory over her own unease: "Soon enough it's true-ooo!"

On "I'll Call You," Lester's buzz-saw guitar gallops around Smith as she reads a fake personal ad—her version of what a truthful guy would say—that sounds like it was placed by a member of the Duke lacrosse team. "Attraction Is Ephemeral," which provides the most complete picture of Smith and what she's about—the way she begins to doubt her own doubts, wondering if she'd be able to spot genuineness in a man even if it were there—is also the most musically moving track on the album. It's the most romantic, too, or rather, it's most explicitly about romance and the yearning for it; though, in typical Mecca Normal fashion, it does so while addressing gender and class inequality, patriarchy, and how they can really ruin a date.

In press releases and online materials, Smith provides links to photos she's used in her dating profile, including shots where she's posing in her underwear and others where she's wearing nothing but the ribbon in her hair. But given how unpleasant *The Observer* makes her dating life out to be, it's hard to argue that the pictures are just convenient exhibitionism—if you're gonna use sex to sell records, you don't usually linger on the vulnerability that intimacy requires.

In the band bio, Smith notes her reluctance to make an album about dating—as evidenced by the fallout late last year over the book *Are Men Necessary?* by *New York Times* columnist Maureen Dowd, romance is a loaded topic among the feminist cognoscenti, perhaps because it's considered unseemly for a feminist to openly admit to wanting something from men (or caring enough to be disappointed with them). Dowd claims that successful men don't want competition from their partners, and thus tend to date or marry down, choosing women who are younger, less educated and less accomplished. Though she makes her argument largely with generalizations, as opposed to Smith's nuanced particulars, both writers are suggesting the same thing—independent women wind up alone.

Smith is forthcoming about the concessions she makes for intimacy. While she holds to her standards with men who aren't good enough, she swallows her pride and sells herself out to others who don't have much idea who she is or much interest in finding out. But her artistic integrity never wavers, and throughout it's clear she knows herself and understands the choices she's making. It's a brave act for her to admit that she quietly shushes the "difficult" parts of herself in order to connect with men: she is airing a common secret of women's lives.

SHOUTING OUT LOUD: THE RAINCOATS

Portland Mercury, **October 2009**

These days, The Raincoats legacy is most often defined by *who* remembered them. In 1992, Kurt Cobain recalled in his *Incestide* liner notes that the British post-punk girl band's debut album had served him as a life-saving device, a reprieve from his depression and boredom; something cool he wished in on. The plaintive mash notes of punk's living Jesus revivified The Raincoats at the time when we needed it most, amid the grunge boom. Underground, there was riot-grrrl salvation and Fugazi, sure, but up top, *cool* was Pearl Jam (not yet sanctified, or anything more than macho qua rebellious) and the best-selling album of the year was Whitney's last stand, *The Bodyguard* soundtrack.

In 1994, when DGC re-issued the trio of records that constituted The Raincoats' discography, the band needed someone to co-sign their artistry. (We can forgive the too-typical fact that the rock star boy's stamp of approval was necessary to accept the genius girl's work.) Cobain was *the* acceptable boy bridge to girl culture, he was part of popping the escape hatch to a better world, his endorsement served as a kind of atonement for the crush of corpogrunge that Nirvana's success accidentally seeded. Then, as now, we needed The Raincoats, to stave off the boredom and depression because there was *still* no other band quite like them.

This week Kill Rock Stars has re-issued The Raincoats' self-titled 1979 debut album on vinyl and the timing couldn't be more perfect. As we are mired in an epic wave of aesthetics-first, and the post-ironic post-punk era hath wrought an inscrutable wave of bands utterly resistant to meaning (swastikas as album "decoration"/neon hippie bullshit, et al.)—*The Raincoats* serves up a reminder that discernible earnestness doesn't automatically signify emo, and having meaning doesn't mean the work isn't open to dynamic interpretation. People keep tending to The Raincoats' legacy with good reason. They were special, yet absolute everygirls, making music that was/is personal, expressive, artful and is full of joy.

Cobain's notes imagined the band perhaps making him a cup of tea, which would be very polite and grandmotherly (though maybe the offer of a spot of tea is what all people expect of British women) coming from a trenchant band. Maybe it's because on the opening track, "Fairytale in the Supermarket," Ana da Silva sings about cups of tea marking time, right after she shouts outs in a derailing, winding, defiant yelp, "No one teaches you how to live!"—she sounds like she figured it out anyhow. She sounds like the kind of woman no one teaches anything.

Listening to the self-titled debut, it's easy to see why they were imagined polite, kind or even doting; rising up from the gnashing pit of punk's nihilism, *The Raincoats* has more PMA than H.R./Bad Brains ever did. They are sunny without being pop, and while they were as rudimentarily skilled as their string-bashing punk peers, there was a sense of a cohesion, another vision of the world—they were out-punking punk, defying its leather/spitting/anarchy trope with art school playfulness and absurdity, down to the sunny, pink drawing of a children's choir right on the cover. They liberated the ultimate girl instrument—the violin—from its school orchestra realm.

Yet, for all of this, *The Raincoats* is often referred to as a harsh, clanging album, the party line usually framing their genius as accidental: girls in the wilderness of their own stuttering hands. The implication being they couldn't have been serious or intentional, sounding as excited and rough and kooky as they did. Punk was full of amateurs, as was post punk (which was more their scene), but girls were always the exception. But as Brilliant Amateurs, they fared a bit better than their compatriots, The Slits, who were so amateur they routinely got compared to wild animals.

Revisiting this album, it's nothing like harsh or shrill. It's filled with space, grace and living. "I am the music inside," they sing on "No Side to Fall In." They knew what they were disregarding and regarding; they were absolutely following their own cues. They sha-la-la'd about their minds, and thinking ("The Void")—they made a record about being real girls knee-deep in the adventure of their young lives. We don't get a love song until deep into side two, "You're a Million," and it's vague at that, a "lover" here and an "I'm yours" pledge and that's about it.

They understood the meaning of covering The Kinks' "Lola" and keeping in all the female gender pronouns. Just the year before, The

Pretenders made their debut with a totally straight (in every way) take on another Kinks song, "Stop Your Sobbing." These girls' "Lola" was less about The Kinks, or homage, and more about exploding all that rock 'n' roll boy seriousness.

The particular amateurishness, the special quality of *The Raincoats*, was willful and girly: it flaunted its gentleness, its otherness, its disregard for virtuosity. They were not naive. *The Raincoats were reactive.* In BBC concert footage from 1980 (YouTube it), singer Ana da Silva sings about the sad dating life of a girl with bad skin, how the world judges and values women—the song does not rock, it trembles—while she clunks two woodblocks together like she's fighting rhythm, resisting the linear path and letting the song disintegrate. Like most of their songs, the bass carries the melody and there is a sing-song to their singing, something is chirping, thudding or skronking in lieu of a solo—none of it obscuring the importance of the words, of what the band really have to say.

The Raincoats are the sound of learning and having fun and making it up as you go along; may they be revivified, rediscovered and reissued infinitely.

MAKING POP FOR CAPITALIST PIGS:
M.I.A.'S МΛҮΛ

Chicago Reader, July 2010

M.I.A.'s third album, МΛҮΛ, arrives piled high with the preconceptions of its audience. But let's set aside Lynn Hirschberg's *New York Times Magazine* profile/takedown and those infamous truffle fries. Let's forget about whatever meaning we extracted (or didn't) from M.I.A.'s "Born Free" video, with its simulated land mines launching little-boy legs sky-high in a cloud of vague polemics and CGI. Let's pretend for a bit we can separate her from her own image, even though in many ways that image is her real art, the daily emanation of a Warholian figure ghost-riding the zeitgeist. Let us simply talk about the thing that made us so interested in Maya Arulpragasam in the first place—her music.

МΛҮΛ is a transmission from the ultra now—an e-mailed camera-phone video compressed till it's cruddy and degenerated, a live-tweeting of capitalist culture's foreclosure proceedings on the tar-blotched shores of American apocalyptica. This is not pleasure pop—it's an allergic reaction to it, an involuntary spasm full of exploding, hissing and banging, all uncomfortably close. For most of its duration, МΛҮΛ is a barrage, mimicking modern information overload. But its crowded, ugly sounds are broken up by scary expanses of what-if—a sort of creepy, hookless drift that gets at her dystopian vision from the opposite angle.

The album starts with the clicking of fingernails on a keyboard, but in lieu of the modem handshake that would follow if this were the '90s, we get drilling and clanging—the sound of something mechanical being pieced together. The first track, "The Message," is less than a minute long, a stage-setting vignette that touches on a topic she's been rolling out in recent interviews, like the cover story of the current *Nylon*—the claim that the CIA monitors, or even invented, Google. Here, as there, she doesn't elaborate much, instead just laying it out as nursery-rhymed fact: "iPhone connects to the Internet, connects to the Google, connects to the government." It's less a well-argued thesis and more the sort of conspiracy theory you might hear in a dorm room after someone's had a few bong rips.

On M ∧ Y∧, M.I.A. doesn't connect dots. She recites lists, mixing brand names with heavier signifiers—CIA, Google, Obama, Allah—in a flat, staccato rap. It's hard to tell whether she's genuinely trying to convince anyone of anything or just using what's become default setting in contemporary fiction and Top 40 hip-hop: relying on the audience's understanding of the connotations of certain brands or products instead of doing any real character development. We get a portrait of a consumer, not of a person, via symbols like champagne, cars, Izods and iPods.

The CIA is of course shorthand for the sins of American power, and that's the focus of this album—America, or M.I.A. in America. (She settled in the Brentwood area of Los Angeles early in 2009.) Her previous albums spanned the world in sound and vision, setting their sights on the havoc globalism wreaks, but M ∧ Y∧ is myopic by comparison. It's as though she's been sidetracked into responding to personal provocations, real or imagined. On "Lovalot," when she tauntingly says, "They told me this was a free country," she sounds like a pissed-off teenager. When she raps "I fight the ones that fight me," it's hard to tell if she's singing as America or as herself.

Despite its statement songs and bombastic production, M ∧ Y∧ often lacks gravitas—it's so overloaded, and tries to do so many things, that it ends up feeling diffused, lightweight. M.I.A. gets on a roll, her music and her message pulling together, and then derails herself with misguided attempts at pop like "Teqkilla," a hook-free tribute to whatever's in the red Solo party cup you're holding in the air. The chorus: "I got sticky sticky / Icky icky weeeed!" (Yes, really.) It feels long after two and a half minutes, and its actual length—six minutes and 20 seconds—represents a grievous overestimation of listener patience. Much of the rest of the middle of the album is just as aimless: "It Iz What It Iz" with its sour sung notes, "It Takes a Muscle" with its treacly synth-reggae uplift and some Auto-Tune to make it sound truly inconsequential.

M ∧ Y∧ gives us a little of everything, and it feels like the potluck it is. Arulpragasam worked piecemeal with six different producers across the album (and more on the editions with bonus tracks.) The cuts with British producer and dubstep poster boy Rusko are interesting—his low-gear grind is pretty dazzling in any setting—but he doesn't compose well for singers. His dark, wub-wubbing electro is so full of detail and WTF twists that it's best taken on its own; despite his awesomely claustrophobic (claustrophonic?) sound, M.I.A.'s Bomb Squad he ain't. The tracks were edited into song forms from recordings of epic jam sessions, and you can tell. With the exceptions of album highlight "Born Free," which samples Suicide's "Ghost Rider," and "XXXO," a straight radio-pop construction, /V\ /\ Y/\ sounds like something roped down from the ether and pasted together.

"You know who I am," she sings on "Steppin Up," and now and then it feels like we do. /V\ /\ Y/\ is as close to a treatise on her personal brand as she's ever gotten—there's a lot more about Arulpragasam, a lot more first person. Or at least as much about M.I.A. as she wishes to be known: a world-weary pop terrorist, a truth-telling Robin Hoodrat here to disabuse of us our first-world ignorance, a siren singer who's seen the rewards of pop-chart success and is alternately burdened with and enchanted by them. "You want me to be somebody who I'm really not," she sings on the hook to "XXXO," but who is she talking to?

Throughout the album, Arulpragasam broadcasts her ID: immigrant, refugee, Pope hater, enemy of the bourgeoisie. She can't leave out the part where she's an international celebrity, even if she'd prefer to ("I don't wanna talk about money, 'cause I got it," she sings on "Born Free"). She is perhaps more than ever doing as Robert Christgau wrote in 2005: making art of her contradictions. They're what make her compelling, and why her rebel-girl image—calculated and genuine, with both halves magnified in the limelight—is so hard to take at face value. M.I.A. confounds us as a pop star and political artist, a slippery shapeshifter moving easily between two positions we've learned to see as incompatible: she's an enemy of America even as she makes pop for Americans.

THERE IS NO GUYVILLE IN SWEDEN: FRIDA HYVÖNEN'S *UNTIL DEATH COMES*

Chicago Reader, **November 2006**

Frida Hyvönen is giving away girl secrets. Her lyrics are confessions, but not the kind you'd hide in a diary or write in a letter you never send—they're the kind of things you'd tell another girl, so the two of you could commiserate about the things boys don't understand, about the private frustration of being a woman in a man's world. Her fearlessness makes me envious, even if I'm a little freaked-out that she just threw the clubhouse door open like that.

Until Death Comes, Hyvönen's first record, came out last year in Sweden and a couple weeks ago here in the States. It could be the Swedish equivalent of Liz Phair's *Exile in Guyville*, full of clear-eyed tales of a hard-thinking girl who hops in and out of bed, drinks some, enjoys herself or doesn't, believes in romance—and clearly knows the price of all of those choices. *Until Death Comes* doesn't titillate like *Guyville* did; Hyvönen doesn't seem too interested in the possibility that a woman singing dirty words could get a rise out of people. Plus, her record's more casual about its autobiographical tone (read: untouched by shame or guilt.) Maybe in Sweden a woman who writes a song about getting drunk and hooking up with a friend doesn't have to handle the topic like a live grenade.

Guest musicians pop up here and there, but for most of the album Hyvönen just accompanies herself on piano, playing with the freshness and unself-consciousness of an amateur who's still in the "I can do anything!" stage of learning an instrument. She tends to alternate like a seesaw between left hand and right, plunking a chord or alternating between two notes. Her voice is plain and bright, and she hasn't got any tricks. But the melodies are very pretty, and despite the sparseness of the music, the lyrics don't overwhelm it; instead the two elements click together, the deft simplicity of one balancing the emotional complexity of the other.

"Once I Was a Serene Teenaged Child" unspools over a distant, resonant waltz figure, and for the first six seconds or so it sounds delicate enough—until Hyvönen matter-of-factly delivers the second line, "Once I felt your cock against my thigh." Soon it's clear that she's taking on an experience I've never heard anyone address in song: the way a girl who wants to be a grown-up woman, yet still be able to stay one of the guys, comes to discover her sexual power over men. "You said a girl like me was torture for you / I didn't know what to do about it and / Somehow it made me feel proud," she sings, then mournfully repeats, "The feeling of pride and the loneliness to it" until the song fades. Her narrative is cool and observational—no one is painted as a victim. Instead she offers an epistemology of sexuality, a time-lapse film of eager and awkward teenage evolution.

Hyvönen sings as a free girl who does as she pleases, her desires no longer husked in naiveté. Her songs are mostly about herself, though some cover the topics of boys and her relationships with them. The album's single, "I Drive My Friend," is about taking a friend to the train station after a night out drinking together, a night that turned romantic. She giddily notices tiny details of their trip and promises to wait "a million years" for him to return, plumes of love rising from her hungover heart, but in the next breath she returns to her own life and its glories: "I have everything / A driver's license / A car and a song to sing." Just to make sure we're clear on her priorities, she repeats the word "sing" 23 times. On "Djuna!" her promise is to herself, to leave the boys behind ("They make me regress and forget my aim") and she pleads with a friend to remind her that life is "a piece of art and a hell to raise."

What makes Hyvönen's songs seem foreign is this combination of unapologetically unsentimental self-regard and head-rush romance. She operates entirely outside the gender dialectics of (American) pop music, where a woman's power is conventionally measured by her ability to lord it over men or reject them, whether she's an R&B balladeer, a singer-songwriter or an indie-rock It Girl. Objectification is a given; the male gaze is what mirrors women's worth back to them.

Hyvönen not only does justice to the complexity of female desires but also allows her men three-dimensional depth—they're not reduced to caricature, either scumbags or superheroes. Men simply don't have the outsize importance to her that would justify demonization or worship—her world doesn't revolve around the axis of one man's erection or attentions. These are the songs of a woman who values her liberty and knows her own worth, whether anybody else does or not.

ACKNOWLEDGEMENTS

Thank you to Tim Kinsella for having such faith and enthusiasm in this book. Thank you to my husband Matthew Hale Clark for helping edit this book and encouraging me to write full time. Thank you to my mom Susie Eaton Hopper for gentle editorial advice and being a model of what a working mom looks like and to my dads for being cool dads and encouraging me to do what I wanted; Steve and Louise Clark for childcare. Thank you to Jude and William for taking such long naps so I could work on these pieces and being the light of my life. This book wouldn't ever have gotten finished if it weren't for Jeanine O'Toole, America's Coolest Babysitter. Props to my agent, Tina Wexler at ICM, for her stewardship, and Dana Meyerson and Kathryn Frazier at Biz3 for their hard work.

Many of these pieces would have never been written were it not for my editors at the *Chicago Reader*—Kiki Yablon, Philip Montoro and Alison True—who fostered me, and gave me many hours of their time so that I might learn how to write. My *Reader* colleagues David Wilcox, Miles Raymer, Liz Armstrong, Anaheed Alani and Leor Galil for being sounding boards as well. A debt of gratitude to Charles Aaron for taking a chance on me back in those fanzine days, and being the guiding light on many of the *SPIN* pieces included here, as well as Rob Harvilla, Steve Kandell and Christopher Weingarten who gave me assignments there and elsewhere. Maura Johnston, Robert Christgau and Brian McManus for Pazz & Jop opps, and Brian especially for saying yes to an R. Kelly piece that no one else wanted to touch, and to Brittany Spanos at the *Voice* and Andrew Gill at WBEZ for crucial support on that piece.

Respect is due to the editorial handiwork of the following: Daniel Sinker at *Punk Planet*, Ezra Ace Caraeff at *Portland Mercury*, Steve Haruch at *Nashville Scene*, Melissa Maerz at *City Pages*, Randall Roberts at *LA Weekly*, Cassie Walker at *Chicago Magazine*, Phoebe Connelly at *The American Prospect*, Julianne Escobedo Shepherd at *Hit It or Quit It* and for talking out ideas that appear in many of the early pieces included here. Special recognition to Kevin Williams at the *Chicago Tribune* for being cool in spite of the fact that I blew deadline every week while working on this book.

The insight of my sister Lauren Redding and the rest of the 'list powered this book: Danielle Henderson, Estelle Tang, Lena Singer, Tavi Gevinson, Amy Rose Spiegel, Gabby Noone, Megan Fredette, Anna Fitzpatrick, JES, Hazel Cills, Arabelle Sicardi, Lola Pellegrino, Emma Straub, Marie Lodi, Jenny Zhang, Stephanie Kuehnert Lewis, Suzy X., Laia Garcia, Brodie Lancaster, Monika Zaleska, Gabi Gregg, Beth Hoeckel, Rose Lichter-Marck, Krista Burton, Naomi Morris, Dylan Tupper Rupert, Pixie Casey, Jamia Wilson, Sandy Honig, Cat Donohue, Tyler Ford, and Maja Demska. How anyone writes a book without a *Rookie* cheerleading crew, I do not know.

A debt of gratitude to my best friend JR Nelson for being DFW for the last 15-ish years, for helping me figure out ideas, filling in my knowledge gaps and accompanying me to almost every show mentioned in this book. Cindy Duckworth for superhuman feats of transcription. James Yates and Yung David Turner for research assistance. Aside from being my friends, the following people helped me dig deeper over the years, and to think harder on pieces included here: Nora Brank, Kate Rose, Morgan Thoryk, David Schied, Michael Catano, Jane Marie, Cali Thornhill DeWitt, Ben Fasman, David Dark, David Bazan, Kevin "Whatever, Kevin" Erickson, Al Burian, Joan Hiller, Sean Daley, Becky Smith, Josh Hooten, Kelly Nothing, Robin and Ian Harris, Marianna Ritchey, Joe Gross, Miles Raymer, Teeter Sperber, and all my colleagues and peers who challenged and inspired me. Thanks to Rob Sheffield, Sara Quin, Teenboss, and Carl Wilson for their acts of generosity. Michael Renaud, David Sampson, Jason Sommer and Zach Dodson for their efforts in making this book come true.

ABOUT THE AUTHOR

Jessica Hopper's music criticism has been included in *Best Music Writing* 2004, 2005, 2007, 2010 and 2011. Her first book, *The Girls Guide to Rocking*, was named one of 2009's Notable Books for Young Readers by the American Library Association. She is Senior Editor at Pitchfork and the Editor-in-Chief of *The Pitchfork Review*. She lives in Chicago with her husband and two young sons.

featherproof BOOKS

*Publishing strange and beautiful fiction and nonfiction
and post-, trans-, and inter-genre tragicomedy.*

Keep Up With The BESTSELLERS!